Dedication

This book is dedicated to my captain for 10 years, Colin Cowdrey,
who was the nicest man I ever had the pleasure of playing cricket alongside.
Like many, I called him 'The Master' and, of all those who helped me during
my cricket career, Colin without doubt provided the inspiration and the
encouragement to go further than I ever thought possible.
Thank you, 'Master'.

Brian Luckhurst
March, 2004

Acknowledgements

The authors would like to thank the following for their help and expertise:
Paul Stannard, Jason Pyne, Anna Harman, Richard Purvis, Ian Patel,
Ian Baker (for photographs on front and back covers, plus pages 6, 35, 84 and 102),
David Robertson, Jon Fordham, John Evans, Bill Marchant, Bob Angell.

The publishers would also like to thank the following for their kind permission to
reproduce certain photographs in this book: Sport & General (pages 35, 40, 68),
Kentish Gazette (p39, 40,78), East Kent Gazette (p21), London Evening Standard
(p94), Victor Pannell (p18), John Hunt (p27), Northern Photos (p69), Bill Smith
(p69), Tom Morris (p87), Robin Humphreys of Press Photographic Services (p8),
The Cricketer (p78), Kent County Cricket Club.

First published in 2004 by KOS Media (Publishing) Limited, Hunstead House,
Nickle, Chartham, Kent CT4 7PE

www.kentonsunday.co.uk

ISBN: 0-9547199-0-5

Printed and bound in Great Britain
by KOS Media Limited. 01227 732223

Boot boy to President

Contents

Introduction

This is the story of what perhaps should be described as the most memorable half-century of my cricketing life: the 50 years I spent, from April 1954, in the employment of Kent County Cricket Club. It has been such a privilege to serve my county.

I would like to begin this introduction by thanking the two people who have made this, my first book, possible. Mark Baldwin of The Times has been a pleasure to work with, while Paul Stannard, the managing director of the Kent on Sunday newspaper, has been the man chiefly responsible for organising and arranging the publication of 'Boot boy to President'.

For a number of years various friends and relatives, and especially my wife Raye and my three boys Tim, Simon and Matthew, have been encouraging (pestering) me to put all my thoughts and memories together in the form of a book. Well, here it is and I sincerely hope that you get as much enjoyment from reading it as I have from putting it together with, of course, a great deal of help from Mark.

I need also to thank my close friend and former playing colleague Derek Underwood for kindly agreeing to write the foreword. To many, including myself, Derek must go down in cricket history as the best left-arm bowler of his type to grace the cricket grounds of the world. His record of 297 Test wickets at an average of 25.83, and 2,465 first-class wickets at 20.28, speaks for itself.

But that is only half the story. It would be difficult to meet a nicer or more modest man than Derek and, I'm prepared to reveal here, he is one of very few men my wife would consider leaving home for! Thank you, 'Deadly', for your contribution to this book.

When, back in April 1954, I left Westlands Secondary School in Sittingbourne to join Kent as a young professional at the age of 15, I could not have begun to imagine the incredible journey that I was about to make. I left school with no qualifications, but fortunately for me I did have a certain amount of sporting potential. Westlands was not a rugby school, but cricket and football, and hockey and athletics, were all strong and encouraged.

Sitting here now, reflecting on this incredible journey that I've experienced, I find it hard to take in all that my cricketing life has contained. I have been to many places that I didn't expect to go to, I have done so many things I never expected to be able to do, and on top of that I've played and worked with some lovely people along the way. And all because at times I managed to get the cricket bat going in the right direction!

I have very few regrets in my life, and have always tried to be positive in my outlook (the glass is always half-full rather than half-empty). One regret, however, is that I came along late for my parents. My mother Ettie was 45 and my father William 53 when I was born. My two sisters, Joan and Verna, were then already 19 and 18 respectively.

In 1962, when I first began to play regularly in the Kent first eleven, I used to take my mother to most home games. However, Mum sadly died in December 1969, aged 75, and it was not until June 1970 that I was selected to play in my first Test match for England. That was something I would have loved her to be able to see, because I know she would have been very proud for me. Although my father never played cricket, I understand that my mother's family (her maiden name was Hammond) at one time used to provide about half the Murston Village Cricket Club's team.

When I first walked through the gates of the St Lawrence Ground at Canterbury as a young professional cricketer, I was just two months past my 15th birthday. How astonished I would have been if, when I left Westlands to go to Kent, my old headmaster Mr Highton had been able to pull me to one side to tell me what the journey that lay ahead was going to include.

"Young Luckhurst," he would have said, "in the next 30 years you are going to represent England, play cricket in South Africa, West Indies, Pakistan, Australia and New Zealand, and you are going to travel around the world several times. Also, because of cricket, you will one day be invited to Buckingham Palace, you will then meet the Queen again at Lord's, and you will also be invited to take afternoon tea with the Queen Mother at Clarence House.

"On top of all that, and because you are going to play in a Kent championship-winning side, the Prime Minister Ted Heath will invite you and the team to have dinner with him at 10 Downing Street. Finally, at the end of what will be a 50-year association with Kent - as player, coach, team manager and administrator - you will be invited to become President of the Kent County Cricket Club."

If Mr Highton, or anyone else, had somehow been able to tell me all that back in April 1954 I would have dismissed it as mere fantasy. But, for that very fortunate young lad of 15, the amazing fact is that it was all eventually going to come true.

Brian Luckhurst
March, 2004

Foreword

By Derek Underwood

For three years - 1969, 1970 and 1971 - Brian Luckhurst was, in my opinion, the premier batsman in England. Moreover, and this applies for the whole of his long and remarkable career, he was the gutsiest cricketer I ever came across.

It is such a pleasure to write this foreword because I hold Brian in high esteem both as a player and as a person. He was a magnificent professional and, for 50 years, has been a credit to himself and to Kent cricket.

Some people might raise their eyebrows at my assessment of him as a batsman, in those peak years of his career. What about Boycott, or Edrich, or - here in Kent - our own Colin Cowdrey?

No, for me, in terms of his run-scoring ability, his determination and his sheer guts, Brian was England's number one at that time - when I feel he overshadowed even the likes of Boycott.

I have shared so many wonderful experiences with Brian, for Kent and for England. We were county teammates for 14 seasons, and it is a lovely coincidence that he opened the batting for Kent for the very first time in the same match that I made my first-class debut - against Yorkshire at Hull in 1963. Even when our respective first-class careers were over, we played together many times in Old

England fixtures, when Brian would always make sure he turned up early to prepare himself as thoroughly as ever in the nets!

But I was also fortunate enough to be able to witness at first hand most of his 21 Test appearances, plus his five unofficial Tests against the Rest of the World in 1970, and I remember being so delighted when, at the age of 31, he was at last selected by England.

We have particularly happy, shared, memories of England's Ashes-winning tour of Australia in 1970-71, as well as Kent's many successes in a golden era. I will also always remember, as evidence of Brian's toughness, how he batted on with a broken finger to score 109 against the Aussies at Melbourne in early 1971.

He suffered the fracture quite early in his innings, but at the tea interval refused to let Bernard Thomas, our physio, treat him. After his innings was finally over, his batting glove had to be cut off him. My first recollection of Brian was of a cricketer who merely stuffed a towel inside his trousers instead of using a proper thigh pad, but here was grit of an even higher order.

Brian fought and fought all the way to achieve what he did. For a batsman who started out with just two shots - the work behind square on the legside, and the punched square cut - he became an accomplished player who responded tremendously to the new challenge of limited-overs cricket in the middle of his career.

In fact, I think the demands of one-day matches helped him enormously in his further development as a batsman, and with typical shrewdness he quickly realised he had to learn new shots. In one-day cricket especially he was Kent's linch pin, and even though he used to frustrate Les Ames by sometimes starting slowly he would always pick up the pace and very often he would see us all the way home. As long as Brian was there, we in the dressing room always felt we were OK!

Talking of Les Ames, I was once officially reprimanded by him for putting a bet on Brian to score a hundred in one of our matches against Surrey at the Oval. But it was a slow, low pitch and at odds of 10-1 it was one of the best £10 investments I ever made!

Brian's character and personality shone through the way he batted. He never gave his wicket away, and he knew his own game intimately. To say he played within his limitations is no criticism - it's yet another compliment for the man we fellow players knew as 'Mr Dependable'.

A lot of our other batsmen at Kent also recognised his full worth to that great team of the late 60's and early 70's, because it was Brian's utter reliability and assurance at the other end which gave players like Mike Denness, Asif Iqbal and John Shepherd the confidence to play their shots.

Brian's story, in Boot boy to President, is fascinating and unique. To be given a professional contract at just over 15 years of age is remarkable enough… but look at everything that has followed it!

I feel very honoured to have been asked to contribute to this book, and very thankful that we were on the same side so often. Why, Brian was even responsible for exactly 100 of my first-class wickets - and those safe hands of his meant that he caught more catches off my bowling than any other outfielder.

Many, many thanks, Brian!

Chapter 1

Lucky Man

When a hard, red missile is coming towards you at almost 100 miles per hour, and when you know that the bowler does not himself have much clue where it is going, your only real thought can be about survival.

In my case, certainly, when facing Jeff Thomson on the rock-like, bouncy pitches of Australia in December 1974, at the age of almost 36, the process of scoring runs was most definitely of secondary importance.

When Thomson jogged deceptively in you had to fight yourself to concentrate on the place on the sightscreen where his bowling hand would let go of the ball. His slinging action meant, unlike with Dennis Lillee, you could not see it as he went through his action. The result was unnerving.

I was never frightened at the crease, but facing Thomson and Lillee at the peak of their powers on England's 1974-75 tour to Australia did make me feel a little bit apprehensive! Thomson, in particular, who was also so outwardly aggressive and not the most pleasant of men on the field, caused me to think only of preserving my wicket and myself. This, don't forget, was still in the era before batting helmets. We went out to bat with just our pads, thigh pad and gloves for protection. There were not even arm guards or chest pads!

There was not that much between their actual pace, if truth be told. Thommo was slightly quicker, and I know he was once timed at 99.7 miles per hour, but the problems he caused were mainly because of the way he banged it in to the pitch - and because his amazing, catapult-style action made it so difficult to pick up the ball.

You have less than half a second to react to the fastest bowlers. In that time, you have to decide whether to play back or forward, whether to leave it or whether to play it, and then of course if you are to attack or defend. At that level, of course, much of what you do is sheer instinct.

Actually, I experienced more problems with Lillee in my Test career, but that was because he was such a fine bowler. His classical action meant you could see the ball better, but then you still had to play it! Years after both our retirements, I saw him at a function in London and he greeted me with the words: "Jeez, how do you keep all your hair, mate!" I replied: "It's because I no longer have to worry about you!" With Thomson, he did not have the same control or skill. On English pitches, he could not just bang it in and get the same results, but in Australian conditions his comparative wildness made him much more of a handful.

In 1974 I just tried to get out of the way of it as the ball exploded past. And, because we did not have helmets, we tried to keep our eyes on it. Batsmen seem to get hit on the head far more now that they have helmets, but we were no braver or more skilful players than are around now. It was just a different time, and that was the way you played.

I faced Frank 'Typhoon' Tyson in only my second first-class match and then Lillee and Thomson in my last two Tests. There were more than 16 years between the two events, and a bit either side of them too. I slept overnight outside the Oval in August 1953, as a cricket-mad 14-year old, to make sure I would get into the ground to watch England regain the Ashes after a 20-year gap and then, in February 1971, soon after my 32nd birthday, I played in a great England team which won back those Ashes again. Yes, I took a few knocks and had to avoid a few high-speed cricket balls along the way, but it was well worth every bump, every bouncer, and every bruise.

*　*　*　*

My first nickname at Kent was 'Nipper', for obvious reasons if you had seen the size of me at the age of 15 and 16. For the vast majority of the past 50 years, however, I have simply been 'Lucky'.

With a surname like mine, of course, that is at first glance merely obvious. Indeed, there are many inside and outside of cricket's dressing rooms who have gloried in far cleverer or more original nicknames than mine. I am not sure, however, if any of theirs has been more appropriate.

Looking back today on my life in cricket, as the newly-appointed Kent president for 2004, I can only shake my head in wonder at how fortunate I have been since the day, in April 1954, that I first walked through the gates of the St Lawrence Ground to begin my first contract as a young professional. I was 15 years and two months old.

Many of you will be familiar with my achievements as a cricketer for Kent and England, and many Kent supporters and members will also not need telling in these pages how immensely proud and happy I am to have been associated with my native county club over six decades.

But this book is about far more important things than how many runs I scored, or how many wickets I took. It is about the unique character of Kent cricket, the great joy it brings to so many people, and the unique nature and qualities of the game of cricket itself.

It is about the way cricket, for me, has opened doors and aided a journey through a life which began in a two-bedroomed terrace house in Sittingbourne - a house with no bathroom and just an outside loo. It is about the many people I have been privileged to get to know, both on and off the field. It is about the growth of a great team, in a great era. It is, too, about a great club and a great way of life.

My story also takes in an England career which, unbelievably for me at the time and still fairly unbelievable when I recall it now, did not start until I was 31.

I count myself fortunate indeed to have been given the chance to be part of a team which won the Ashes in Australia - a sporting achievement which only the passage of history can put into proper context. In modern terms, I suppose, it's a bit like an England rugby team beating the Australians in Australia to win their World Cup.

Yet if that, and Kent's many successes in a golden era, represented the playing pinnacles of my career, then there have been other peaks too. Perhaps not so glaringly visible, but equally satisfying. Like coaching young players who went on to build on Kent's best cricketing traditions, like contributing in latter years to the way the club has been improved and run, and now by being able to make a contribution as my county's president.

I have been very fortunate, moreover, in having had the support of a succession of cricket people who believed in me. You will already have seen that this book is dedicated to Colin Cowdrey, or Lord Cowdrey of Tonbridge as he became before he sadly passed away in December, 2000. That is in large part because of the inspiration he gave me to strive for goals on the cricket field that I never believed was possible for the very moderate cricketer - in terms of natural ability - that I always knew I was.

Yet I very nearly did not have a cricket career of any note at all, and that I did is almost certainly down to just one man - the late Colin Page.

When I returned from my two years of National Service in July 1960, after having made my first three first-class appearances as a 19-year old all-rounder just before my call-up in the summer of 1958, I found I had stagnated as a cricketer.

Yes, I had played a lot of cricket while I was in the Army - including, amazingly, two matches for Pembrokeshire (more about that later!) - but my performances back in the county second XI towards the end of the 1960 season, and then throughout the 1961 summer, suggested that my dream of becoming a fully-fledged county professional was indeed mere wishful thinking.

He never confirmed this to me himself, and I would never have embarrassed him by asking about it, but I suspect very strongly indeed that Colin Page was the reason that the Kent committee chose to ignore the evidence of the 1961 season and offer me yet another one-year contract for 1962.

Even allowing for my two-year absence, serving in the Royal Artillery, I had been at Kent for six full seasons by then, plus another half of one, and at 22 I was fast running out of time.

It was Page, then Kent's second team coach, who bought me another precious six months of opportunity on the field of play - and then, early in the 1962 season itself, it was Colin who yet again put his neck on the block for me by recommending me for a return to the first team after an absence of almost four, long, years. Colin's championing of me was even more remarkable on that occasion, at the beginning of the week that was to change my life, because his recommendation for my promotion came on the back of me bagging a pair in my previous appearance for the second XI !

Perhaps he sensed my almost desperate determination to do well, or my determination to make the absolute best of what I had got. Who knows? But Colin was as good a judge of a cricketer, and character, that I've ever known, and he was willing to give me a chance. And, whoever you are, and whatever your career path, everyone needs a chance.

Yet would I ever have had a career in cricket at all but for two of my schoolmasters in Sittingbourne, my form teachers at Murston Primary School and then Westlands Secondary School? Their names, respectively, were Doug Wallace and Denis Jarrett, and the next chapter should be dedicated to them.

They helped me on to the first rungs of cricket's ladder, but it was another Sittingbourne man who gave me the early guidance and confidence to start climbing.

Claude Lewis is perhaps remembered most by Kent supporters as the county's trusty scorer for many of the years preceding the current incumbent, Jack Foley. But he was also a fine slow left-arm spinner in his playing days, whose opportunities had been limited largely by the War and by the presence at Kent of the great Doug Wright, and he was by the early 1950's the county coach. What is more, he lived about 600 yards away from our house in Sittingbourne.

I often think it was meant to be that Claude was, literally, on hand to drive me up to Kent winter nets at Eltham every Thursday afternoon, in the six months before I joined the staff, and that it was also more than a coincidence that I, too, began my cricketing life as predominantly a slow left-arm spinner. How else can you explain great good fortune like that?

When I then did join Kent as a young professional, it was still Claude who used to pick me up from home and drive me off to work - whether it was to nets or

HOUSE OF
COMMONS

Brian Luckhurst

THE TEST AND COUNTY CRICKET BOARD SELECTION
SUB-COMMITTEE

request you to be available to play, if selected, for

ENGLAND

v.

AUSTRALIA

at   Trent Bridge

on   13th – 18th July, 1972

R.S.V.P.
The Secretary of the T.C.C.B.

(Conditions of Acceptance and Notes and Instructions for Test Matches attached)

HOUSE OF LORDS

Brian Luckhurst

ADMIT

Mr. B. W. Luckhurst

to Dinner at 10, Downing Street, Whitehall

on   18 DEC 1973

In the event of acceptance, please bring this card, which
must be presented at the door.

The Comptroller of the Household
to
Queen Elizabeth the Queen Mother
is commanded by Her Majesty to invite
Mr. Brian Luckhurst
to Clarence House
on Sunday 25th June 1972

A reply is requested to The Comptroller to
Her Majesty Queen Elizabeth The Queen Mother,
Clarence House, St. James's, London, s.w.1.

**A few places that I didn't expect to visit,
and a few people I didn't expect to meet**

**The man to whom I owe a great debt. Colin Page,
a great figure in the history of Kent cricket**

daily chores at Canterbury, or matches home or away. I can still remember those many journeys, up and down the A2, in his Standard 8 car - registration number BFN 600!

It was on one of those journeys in Claude's car, too, on the evening of August 1, 1957, that I received the single most important piece of encouragement of my entire cricket career.

I was 18 at the time, and two-thirds of the way through a season in which I was to take a total of 88 wickets at an average of 13.5 for the second XI and the Club & Ground team. I was also beginning to make a mark at last with the bat, and my progress was clearly being monitored by an old Kent cricketer called Bill Fairservice, who had taken 853 first-class wickets in 301 appearances for the county between 1902 and 1921 and who had played in the Kent championship-winning sides of 1906, 1909, 1910 and 1913.

Bill was by then in his late 70's but he was the Kent second XI scorer and someone to be respected. Claude was also giving him a lift home from our game against Middlesex seconds at Folkestone, and I was sitting in the back of the car when Bill turned to me and congratulated me on my performance in the two-day match.

It had been an exciting finish, with a low-scoring game ending in a draw as we failed by just one run to reach a target of 137 in 38 overs. Batting at number seven, I was nine not out at the finish, in a total of 135-9, with my ninth wicket partner having been run out off the final ball trying for the extra run that would have earned us a tie. In the rest of the match I had also scored a first innings unbeaten 53 and had taken 2-32 and then 5-51.

I thanked Bill for his kind words, but he then said and did something which I have never forgotten. He said: "I know you are still a young lad, Brian, and wondering if you are good enough for a future in this game. Well, you might not get picked in the first team this summer, but I've got a feeling that one day soon you will be needing one of these…" And, with that, he produced an old Kent members' tie from out of his pocket - his own tie, of course - and told me to take it. As I knew, it was traditional to be given one of those ties as a player only once you had made three first-class appearances for the club.

I was speechless, but I also cannot begin to describe even now - almost 50 years later - what Bill's words meant to that particular young hopeful. It gave me such a boost in confidence to know that he, as a successful former player and also someone other than Claude, had decided I would make it.

When, just under 12 months later, I arrived at New Road to make my first-class debut in a county championship match against Worcestershire, I took with me old Bill Fairservice's tie. And then, a week or so later when I played my third first-class match for Kent, I made sure that I actually wore it. I was so proud, and today, though it is now a bit worn around the edges, it is still one of my most treasured possessions.

All in all, you see, I really have been so very lucky.

Chapter 2
The Making of a Cricketer

Some cricketers are indeed born, such is their abundance of natural ability. Others, like myself, are most definitely made.

I never played for any Kent Schools representative teams, or anything like that, but I did have a talent for all ball games and - of course - there has to be some amount of natural aptitude if you are to excel at any particular sport.

But I have always said that being a successful professional sportsman is more than 50 per cent about application, hard work, determination, mental strength, your make-up as a person and sheer want, and less than 50 per cent about talent. There are always exceptions to every rule, of course - geniuses like Colin Cowdrey and David Gower, for instance, but in most other cases I will stand by my belief.

Some people have said to me that I must have been extremely talented to be given a professional contract at the age of just 15, and I suppose my teenage bowling ability must have stood out. Even in those days, when the turnover rate of young players year-to-year was extremely high, you were only given coveted things like contracts if the hardened old professionals who made such decisions thought that you had something to offer.

There may have been another reason, too, however. Because of Claude Lewis being from Sittingbourne like me, and because he had also been a slow left arm spinner like me, I think there was a big element of him taking me under his wing. He was certainly my first cricketing mentor and, throughout my subsequent career and even when he had finished as county coach and become the club's scorer, he was always the first person I went to if I was experiencing a sticky patch with my technique.

But the real truth of the matter, in relation to my success as a cricketer, is that not even Claude could have predicted - back in my early years on the Kent staff - that here was a player who was going to be good enough to open the innings for Kent and England and score 48 first-class centuries. I was a number 11 batsman for the second XI for a number of years, remember, and it was very much as a bowling all-rounder - batting at number seven - that I got to make my first team debut in 1958.

Again, looking back, it is quite remarkable to me that anyone could have given such an opportunity to a little lad of 15, especially as the natural loop that young spin bowlers have almost always disappears when they get taller and older. But even that is not as remarkable as the fact that it is as an opening batsman that I made a lasting success of the game. If you had told me at 19, or even at 23 when I got back into the Kent first team, that I would go on to score those 48 first-class hundreds - four of which would be in Tests - but take only 64 first-class wickets, I would not have believed it.

As a kid, I was mad on both football and cricket, and it would be fair to say that playing sport always came out a long way ahead of studying at school. I wasn't very good in the classroom, but in the playground or out on the playing fields… well, that was altogether more stimulating and exciting.

If the cap fits... my early teens featured playing cricket at Westlands School in Sittingbourne

There was also time to fit in captaining the Westlands School football team

A rare photograph of me before cricket played a part in my life!

I was like so many other boys of that generation, in that my first experience of playing sport came in the playground. Cricket was the summer sport, without question, and my first bat was a rough piece of wood and my first ball was a grubby old tennis ball. We chalked the stumps on to a wall in the playground, and we played through every break, and even after school when other kids were going home! My first 200 was made in the playground, because there were no boundaries - you just hit it as far as you could and kept on running while someone went to fetch it!

Doug Wallace was my form teacher at Murston Primary School, and he also looked after the school's cricket team. I remember him being very keen on the game, which was marvellous for us boys, and it was down to Mr Wallace that I received the first official recognition of my cricket ability.

Playing in a school match on a pitch cut out on the Gore Court outfield, I took 7-20 and then scored an unbeaten 80 (out of 86 without loss!) in a 10-wicket win against Holy Trinity. Of course, I was pleased with myself, but Mr Wallace thought my performance was worthy of special merit. He entered me into a competition that was being run every month in the Star newspaper in London, specifically aimed at young cricketers.

They were impressed with the enclosed scorecard of the match, and I was duly given that month's award. It was a great fillip for the school, of course, but it did even more for me. Not only was there a feeling awakened in me that cricket was something I really could be good at, but my prize was a brand new cricket bat!

I can still remember now going up to London on the train with my mother, clutching the voucher that had been sent to me and which I was to exchange for the bat at Stuart Surridge's cricket shop. It was my first trip to London, too, and that bat was the very first piece of cricket equipment that I had owned.

Can you imagine what winning that bat, and having to go up to London to collect it, meant to a scrawny 12-year old who had never been outside of Sittingbourne? It inspired me, it fired me, and all I wanted to do after that was play cricket... and more cricket.

Apart from playing and practising, I also went to watch Kent play a few times - cycling the 18 miles to Canterbury, and back again, for the privilege. It was Arthur Fagg and Les Todd who I first watched opening the Kent innings in those days.

In August 1953, aged 14, I also went up on the train to London to see England beat Australia at the Oval to win back the Ashes. The last time England had owned the little urn was in 1932-33, after Douglas Jardine's infamous 'Bodyline' tour, and so this was an incredibly exciting occasion. What I did not know at the time, of course, and what I would never even have dreamed, was that I was going to be in the England team which regained them in 1970-71 after the Ashes had been lost again in Australia in 1958-59.

What a commentary it is on my boyhood days, by the way, that my close friend Roger Corden and I were in absolutely no danger at all when we slept in the streets outside the Oval in order to be there in the morning when the gates opened for that historic last day! Roger had been my opening partner when I made the 80 not out two summers earlier to win my bat and travel up to London for the first time. Now we both went up from Sittingbourne to Victoria Station the evening before, and got the bus down Vauxhall Bridge Road before settling in to make sure we were first in the queue. And it was well worth the wait to see Denis Compton score the winning runs and cheer the return of the Ashes to their rightful owners!

By then I was also in my second season with the Murston Village Cricket Club, and I was the only real youngster in a team run by Harold Gilbert. He was the man who did everything that has to be done to run a village team, and my mother's family knew him well. I batted very low in the order, but bowled my left-arm spinners regularly. I also played for my school year team at Westlands Secondary School, but it was in the winter of 1953-54 that my cricket career shot forward.

Denis Jarrett, my form master at Westlands, was chiefly responsible for this acceleration. Neville Christopherson, then the Kent secretary, had been instructed by the county committee to write to all Kent's schools during the winter asking for recommendations of any young cricketing talent. The county team, at that time, was in a state of flux with several big name players (notably Les Ames, Les Todd and Bryan Valentine) having all quite recently retired. The team was being carried by the likes of Doug Wright, Godfrey Evans and Arthur Fagg, and was in dire need of some new young blood.

And so it was that Kent officials were told about a 14-year old young lad called Luckhurst, from Sittingbourne, who bowled promising left-arm spinners and also batted a bit as a right-hander. Mr Jarrett soon got a letter back from Kent, inviting me for a trial! That day, after I had been told this remarkable news, Mr Jarrett took me along to the school library and made me read up everything about spin bowling in the MCC Coaching Manual. That, I suppose, was my first coaching lesson!

The real thing, however, was soon upon me. Claude Lewis, the Kent coach who lived nearby in Sittingbourne, but who I had not then met, was detailed to pick me up at 2pm on the following Thursday afternoon… and take me to bowl at some Kent players in the county's only indoor nets at Eltham Baths.

I remember very little about that first net session, against professional batsmen, except that Arthur Phebey was one of the Kent players I bowled to - and that I felt quite comfortable. Perhaps it was the naivety of youth, or the excitement of the occasion, but I didn't feel overawed by what was happening to me. Maybe that was the first big step I took towards being offered my first Kent contract just six months later!

All I know is that, from that day, I was asked to attend the Eltham nets every single Thursday. Claude would pick me up outside the school gates at 2pm prompt, and after the hour and a half's drive up to South-East London I would bowl and bowl until it was time to leave again. We wouldn't get home until 8pm or 9pm, but I didn't mind. I was practising my cricket, against real cricketers, and I was also getting the benefit of all Claude's advice as we drove up and down the A2. It made me feel good, too, that every Thursday I was granted an afternoon off school - my classmates were envious, and I think this was another early 'achievement' which convinced me that cricket might do great things for me.

As I have said, though, I was never selected for any Kent Schools team during my time at Murston or Westlands, yet my learning curve was a pretty steep one once I got into men's cricket at the age of 13 (even though it was village cricket) and then started to go to Kent nets. I don't remember doing anything spectacular with ball or bat in the 1952 and 1953 summers, but I was gaining in experience all the time - and, looking back, that was the important thing.

It was Claude Lewis who, at the end of the 1953-54 winter coaching sessions, invited me to take part in Kent's full-scale Easter coaching classes at Canterbury. Things were about to happen very fast indeed.

I was due to leave school in April 1954, and I had already taken the Dockyard

Colin Cowdrey presents prizes to pupils at Westlands School in October 1968. I am on the far right, and on the extreme left are Headmaster Denis Jarrett, Claude Lewis and Bob Wilson - all fellow Sittingbourne men

Arthur Phebey, who was the first senior player that I can remember bowling at as a fourteen year old in the nets at Eltham Baths

Entrance Exam at Chatham. There were 32 apprenticeships available, for trades such as carpentry and plumbing, and I had somehow managed to come second in the exam. The others who took that exam couldn't have been the brightest!

So, I had a job waiting for me at Chatham Dockyard when Kent decided - on the strength of my winter and Easter net performances - to offer me a three-month trial. Claude Lewis came round to our house, and he sat with me and my Mum and Dad in the front room to discuss the situation.

I didn't say much, and I wasn't asked to say much! But Dad was concerned that a three-month trial would mean a very precarious existence for me, and told Claude that he felt I should be offered a whole season. He underlined the fact that I had a job at the Dockyard to go to, if I didn't go to Canterbury, and that this was quite a lot to give up for a mere three-month deal. Did Kent really want me as a young professional, or not?

Well, his reasoning clearly paid off. Claude reported back to the Kent committee, and very soon I was the happy recipient of another offer - this time for a whole six months! I was off to be a professional cricketer, just two months beyond my 15th birthday.

Looking back now, more than half a lifetime away, it was not only my age that made all this so crazy. I had never batted in the nets at Eltham, or at Canterbury at Easter, because it was then only the senior batsmen who practised batting. There had been no fielding practice, either. I was there simply to bowl. But how could I have been judged on that alone? Yes, it is true that this was merely the system in that era - but it was still ridiculous that a 15-year old boy, who in truth had never really done anything to warrant it, had suddenly become a professional cricketer.

Even at 18 or 19, it is sometimes difficult to predict the best cricketers. John Snow and Derek Shackleton, for instance, both began their county careers as batsmen - before going on to be two of the finest bowlers that England has produced since the War. David Smith, of Surrey, started out as a fiery fast bowler who batted at number 11 - but ended up opening the batting for England after he was forced to give up his bowling because of injury. Mark Richardson, the current and very successful New Zealand opener, started his first-class career as a slow left-armer and tailender. And what about Kent's own Alan Knott? He joined the Kent staff as an off-spinner!

Back in April 1954, though, all this was the last thing on my mind. I had signed for Kent, on four pounds and ten shillings per week, and I was ecstatic. Forget my age, I was on the staff alongside stars of English cricket like Godfrey Evans and Colin Cowdrey and Doug Wright. Better than that, I sometimes got to speak to them - let alone bowl at them!

When you are 15, of course, you don't really think about what is happening to you - it is just a matter of doing what's in front of you. That was me at 15, and if I'm brutally honest I also think that I probably played a part in talking my parents into it because, at that stage of my life, I was very much the little spoilt brat. I had two sisters who were substantially older than me, remember, and I was doted on. And if young Brian wanted to go and play for Kent... well, that's what I was allowed to do!

My mother, nevertheless, was also very keen for me to be a cricketer. She came from a family in which cricket was a big thing, whereas I think my father really didn't know enough about it to argue! I'm sure, too, that Claude's belief in me helped to make up their minds that I should be given the opportunity. He clearly thought I looked the part, but what else could he have based his belief on? At 15, I still had a lot of growing up to do - both physically and as a person.

At that stage I had hardly been outside of Kent - except those trips to London -

and as a family we had only ever had one holiday, to Cliftonville near Margate. I had to cycle 40 miles to get there, too, because we didn't have a car. And when I joined the Kent staff, I distinctly remember the pleasure of the first soaks I had in the hot bath in the pavilion dressing room. We youngsters usually had to use the cold showers in the Colts Room, but it was special when you got to use the deep dressing room baths. Especially for me, because all I had been used to at home was a tin bath in front of the fire on a Friday night!

I can also recall, in my first summer at Canterbury, going with some other players into a restaurant for the first time in my life. I was OK when there was only one knife and fork beside the plate - but what did you do when there was more than one of each?

What was it about me, then, that enabled me to make it as a cricketer? As I've said, in terms of natural ability I was very limited. My success came about from sheer hard work, and I've seen so many players with more natural talent fall by the wayside.

I suppose Claude, and perhaps others at Kent, saw in me an attitude and willingness to work hard that they knew would carry me along. Without me being aware of it at the time, I expect they also noticed that I had excellent ability in respect of temperament, and approach to the job in hand. In English cricket of the 1950's, though, there was less attention paid to the technical side of coaching - indeed, people like Les Ames didn't actually believe in coaching at all. In Les' eyes, you either had 'it' or you didn't; you either worked it out for yourself, or you failed.

With the benefit of hindsight, too, I can appreciate that my survival in those early months at Kent had a lot to do with the fact that I was predominantly being judged and assessed as a bowler. First, bowling is more natural than batting, and secondly as a bowler you have at least six chances to get it right before you can be taken off. As a batsman, you might only get one chance!

Whatever, this was but the start of my long cricketing journey and I was determined to do all in my power to justify Kent's faith in me. I loved everything to do with cricket, and I had six months to show what I could do. Perhaps, at the end of it, I might be given a £25 winter retainer and then another summer contract in 1955. Life was exciting, and I threw myself into it with a youthful vigour.

When I look back on the cricketer I was at the start of my professional career, there is little I can recognise in terms of the cricketer I was to become. But what I do still recognise most clearly is that I possessed a desire to succeed which always drove me on.

Even towards the end of a first team career at Kent which spanned 15 seasons, I had the same inner voice telling me to work hard and never relax. I saw a lot of young players come and go during my playing days - cricketers who were young and hopeful like I had been.

I always shook them by the hand, and I always wished them well. And then I said to myself: "If you want to play for Kent then there are 10 other places in the team for you to play in. But you're not having my place. No, not my place".

Chapter 3
Boot Boy

I cannot remember who owned the first pair of boots I cleaned as a young Kent professional. Perhaps they belonged to Godfrey Evans, or Doug Wright, or Arthur Fagg. All I know is that I ended up cleaning an awful lot of boots!

There were two of us who joined the Kent staff as youngsters in April 1954. The other new 'boot boy' was Stuart Knight, from Horsmonden, who was then 17. He was an off-spinning all-rounder and joined initially on the three-month trial terms that my father had turned down when they were offered to me.

Stuart, in fact, made it through several seasons on the staff before becoming one of the majority: that is, those who did not go on to forge fully-fledged professional careers. Sport at professional level is a savage business at the best of times, but at Kent in the 1950's there was a brutal turnover in terms of young players and my first task (apart from cleaning the boots) was to start to learn my trade... and learn fast.

In that 1954 season I played four times for the second XI, scoring only two runs from four innings (one was a nought not out!) but picking up seven wickets from a total of 41.5 overs at an average of 27.28. For the Club and Ground XI, however, I played in 21 matches and took 38 wickets from 178.5 overs at an average of just 13.76. My highest score with the bat, in four innings that produced 31 runs (three of them not out) was 11.

The bottom line, which was far more important than bare figures - however tidy - was that I had impressed those that mattered enough to be offered another year's contract for 1955. At that age a year is a long time, and when in September I was put on a winter retainer and told I would be on the staff again the following summer it felt like a huge reward for my efforts.

In a way, I suppose it was. I had survived my 'apprentice' summer, and if truth be told I had relished it. All I wanted to do was play cricket, and even if I was doing the chores I was still on a cricket ground and rubbing shoulders with real cricketers. I've also always enjoyed fielding, and fielding practice, unlike some. Fielding duty, to help out the senior players' practice was, therefore, something I liked to do. If there was a ball to be caught, or thrown, then I was happy. I was in love with cricket, in all its infinite variety.

I had been given the opportunity to be a professional cricketer because I had an ability to bowl a ball, but also because I had the chance to get better. And getting better was something I desperately wanted to do.

Being a gopher around the St Lawrence Ground, or at whatever other home ground I was detailed to be on duty, was merely part of the deal. It was part of growing up, as a cricketer, to work and help the first team. You bowled a lot in the nets at them too, of course, but you also did all manner of odd jobs.

For the first few years of my Kent career I was, for most of the time it seemed, the dressing room attendant. I was expected to be available whenever one of the senior players wanted something, or wanted an errand run. For a week of back-to-back championship matches, for instance, that meant being around every day except Sunday (on which there was no cricket in those days) and often also meant working deep into the evenings when all the players had left.

During the day it was mainly a question of running the errands and clearing up the lunches, and then the teas. At the close of play, once everyone had bathed and changed, I had to clear up the dressing room as well. Besides a general clean around, I also had to deal with the pads… and boots.

If any pads had been left on the middle of the dressing room floor it meant that they needed cleaning, with perhaps a little whitener applied. The boots had to be collected up, wiped clean with a damp cloth and dried off with a dry cloth. Each boot then needed a fresh coat of whitener, which I put on with a paint brush. Once they were all done, it was required that each pair was put back under the part of the dressing room bench which ' belonged' to their respective owners.

I can vividly remember, in 1962, when I played my first championship game at Canterbury, the tingling feeling of arriving at the ground on the second morning of the match and rushing up to the dressing room to see if MY boots had been cleaned and put back in their correct place. Don't laugh. It was a big moment for me, you see, to be able to put my own boots out for cleaning. It meant I'd nearly made it.

One of the other jobs I sometimes had to help out with during play was the operation of the big scoreboard at what is now the Les Ames Stand end of the St Lawrence Ground. You were given a long pole with a hook on the end in order to take off the big metal numbers when the scores changed and replace them with the right ones. Once, however, I didn't catch hold of the number properly with the hook and it fell down and stuck upright in the grass below. It could have decapitated someone if they had been walking beneath me.

On other occasions I well recall myself and other youngsters having to put out 1800 stacked seats that had to be taken off a lorry and carried, four at a time, into the Frank Woolley Stand. Sometimes, too, we had to help the groundstaff to push the heavy roller up and down the pitch before the start of an innings.

It is not wrong that current young players don't have to go through the sort of working 'apprenticeship' that I and so many others had to do, but by the same token I can't help feeling that something is missing now from what is expected of the aspiring young cricketer.

Getting to rub shoulders constantly with the top players - who, of course, I always used to refer to as Mr Evans, Mr Cowdrey, Mr Fagg and so on - gave you a valuable insight into how they prepared themselves for cricket, how they talked about the game, and how they conducted themselves in public and private.

Just being around them, from day to day, also gave you a stronger urge to become part of their world. They had real status, and as a youngster you could only dream of having a similar stature yourself. But, as far away as you were from being a senior player like them, it was still all there in front of you - you could feel it, touch it almost, and you ended up wanting it even more than ever.

The senior players might have given you the odd flea in your ear - such as the time that fast bowler Fred Ridgway refused to give me the traditional two-shilling tip because he decided I had not cleaned his boots properly - but overall they appreciated your efforts on their behalf. They had almost all been boot boys themselves at some stage, of course, and I certainly didn't consider myself hard done by to be a boot boy too.

Part of growing up as a young player at Kent, and indeed at other counties, was this requirement for you to do the chores. It was not questioned. That was your

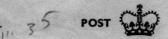

POST OFFICE
TELEGRAM

ON 150

Charges to pay
_____ s. _____ d.
RECEIVED

No._____
OFFICE STAMP

Prefix. Time handed in. Office of Origin and Service Instructions. Words.

At_____ m

From 1796 10.55 ORPINGTON XW 19

By

To_____ m

-OVERNIGHT LUCKHURST KENT ELEVEN WORCESTER COUNTY

CRICKET GROUND WORCESTER

= EVERY GOOD WISH FOR SUCCESS IN YOUR FIRST

MATCH = COWDREY + + ᛭ XW 0

For free repetition of doubtful words telephone "TELEGRAMS ENQUIRY" or call, with this form B or C
at office of delivery. Other enquiries should be accompanied by this form, and, if possible, the envelope. C

Colin Cowdrey, who was playing in a Test match for England, still found the time to wish me well on my first-class debut at New Road, Worcester, in 1958

The proud possessor of a Kent second XI sweater

job, and that was the way things were.

Indeed, being a boot boy as a young professional certainly helped to make me the cricketer I became. It was part of making you more determined to get better, and to learn how to get better. And you learned, in that system, by watching and playing, by practising and by learning to understand your own game. You constantly worked at it, if you wanted to get on, and any direct technical coaching you received was designed to start you off - to get you on the right track. After that, it was down to you.

Having belief in your own ability, and backing yourself to get something done, is a crucial part of learning to become a professional sportsman. The best way to gain that self-belief, of course, is to understand what you are trying to achieve… and how best to achieve it.

When you are right at the start of your journey, however, you often need a bit of good fortune or the impetus of a good early performance. True belief comes from knowing, really knowing, that you can offer something. I was lucky enough to get the initial encouragement of what the Kent Yearbook of 1955 records as a 10-wicket haul on my first day as a Kent player… in two separate matches!

In the Yearbook it is recorded that, on May 12 1954, I played in a Kent second XI team which beat United Hospitals by 60 runs at Canterbury, and took 4-38 from 8.5 overs. But, also on May 12, I scored 10 not out and then snapped up 6-60 from 12.5 overs as the Kent Club and Ground XI defeated the Woolwich Polytechnic Union by seven runs at Eltham Well Hall. What a prospect this boy must have been!

I'd like to say that I can clearly remember the details of both games - and I'd like most of all to be able to say that I did star in two separate matches on the same day! Sadly, our research for this book uncovered the fact that this amusing little 'story' is, hardly surprisingly, incorrect.

The game against United Hospitals actually took place on May 11, 1954, despite what it says in that sacrosanct Kent Yearbook. What this all means, nevertheless, and therefore what this book can now reveal (after 50 years!) is that my Kent second XI debut occurred when I was 15 years and 95 - not 96 - days old!

A month later, and no doubt buoyed up by these early successes, I made my Kent second XI championship debut (at 15 years and four months of age) in a two-day game against Essex seconds on June 16-17 at Walthamstow. We lost by seven wickets, and batting at number 10 I scored just 0 and 2. With the ball, and given a bowl in just one Essex innings, I went for 27 runs off four overs, but I did get a wicket. An unfortunate gentleman by the name of WG Spencer was caught by Tony Woollett.

I also played in two more second XI championship fixtures, against Middlesex at Gravesend on June 30-July 1 and then away to Wiltshire at Marlborough College on August 20-21. I was down at number 11 in both these drawn games, not getting to the crease at all against Middlesex and scoring 0 not out against Wiltshire. I picked up 1-82 from 14 overs at Gravesend, and 1-36 from 12 at Marlborough. Playing in the Kent team against Middlesex were also Stuart Leary, Alan Dixon, Derek Ufton and George Downton. What experiences for a young lad who had hardly ever been out of Sittingbourne!

Most of my memories of that first 1954 season are clouded by the mists of time, I'm afraid, but there are two specific matches that I do recall. The first was on June 22, in a Club and Ground fixture against Catford Cricket Club. Although I can't actually remember taking 3-0 from 2.3 overs to finish off a Catford innings wrecked by Folkestone's John Spanswick returning figures of 8-6-7-7 with the new ball, I do clearly recollect the former Kent opener Les Todd playing for Catford and asking me to move from my close-in position at short leg because my shadow was encroaching on to the pitch! Then, on July 2, I remember being pleased with myself for taking 5-41, again for the Club and Ground team, when we met the Kent County Constabulary at their Sutton Road ground in Maidstone!

In 1955 and 1956 I made steady, if unspectacular, progress. My second XI and Club and Ground XI figures for both those seasons show that I was a dependable bowler, but also someone who hardly ever got a decent bat!

I took 26 wickets in 1955 and made exactly 100 runs from 14 innings, with a top score of 22, while in the summer of 1956 I only batted nine times. In addition to my 22 wickets, however, I scored unbeaten innings of 24, 10 and 39 in my only three opportunities to bat in the second XI championship. Here, at the age of 17, was the first evidence of an emerging ability to score runs... and to occupy the crease!

It was in 1957 that I suddenly made significant strides towards my goal of becoming a first XI player. My 48 wickets for the second XI were taken at 17.96 runs apiece, and with the bat I made 311 runs overall from 21 innings - which included that unbeaten 53 at Folkestone which earned me old Bill Fairservice's tie.

My 364.3 second XI overs were almost 100 more than anyone else bowled, while in Club and Ground matches I bagged another 40 wickets, this time at the startlingly low average of 8.35. Moreover, my batting average for the Club and Ground team was 105.33, courtesy of eight not outs from 11 innings! I was clearly learning not to throw away my wicket, but it was plainly those 88 wickets with the ball that made 1957 a breakthrough season in my young cricketing life.

By the start of the 1958 summer I was putting in performances which underlined my development into an all-rounder. I scored a hundred for the Club and Ground XI, my first in a Kent shirt, and top-scored with 80 as I totalled 473 runs from 26 innings for the second XI. But it was on July 16, at New Road in Worcester, that I fulfilled the first part of my dream to become a fully-fledged county cricketer. It was a proud day for me.

Colin Cowdrey was away on England Test duty, and John Pretlove was captaining the side. On a rain-affected opening day, my first-class career proper began when, at 71-4 in our first innings, Jack Pettiford was dismissed and I went in at number six to join Stuart Leary with the pavilion clock showing 6.13pm. Surviving a tense final 17 minutes of the day, I went on to bat for another 45 minutes the following morning before being the last man out for 23 - bowled by John Aldridge. We were all out for only 128, but I was satisfied enough with my own first effort. Sadly, Worcestershire went on to win the game by eight wickets, and I was bowled for just 11 by Jack Flavell in our second innings. My debut game, however, had - for me - a memorable ending. With match all but over, I was finally thrown the ball and, in a spell of 7-3-9-1, I had Don Kenyon caught behind the wicket by Tony Catt as he tried to cut a long hop outside off stump!

I had also caught Ron Headley, off Dave Halfyard's bowling, during the Worcestershire first innings, so it was a happy enough 19-year old who travelled off that afternoon to Northampton, where my second first-class match was to begin the very next day.

July 19 did not begin so badly, either, with Raman Subba Row pushing forward and gloving a catch to Leary at short leg in my first innings spell of 11-4-27-1. Two wickets to my name already - and two Test players! Things, however, then took a considerable turn for the worse with me getting out for 1 and 0 as Kent tumbled to defeat by an innings and 156 runs. The only positive was that I had managed to see off a few thunderbolts from Frank Tyson - indeed, scoring my single off him with a glance to fine leg - before being castled by that clever chinamen and googly bowler George Tribe. In our second innings I was bowled by Jack Manning, and the other vivid memory I have of that match was the sight of Bob Wilson being carried off the field after being hit in the box by a delivery from Albert Lightfoot!

That incident would not have done much for the confidence of young Luckhurst, who at the time was waiting to bat, but I nevertheless managed to hold on to my place for the next match, which was a return fixture with Worcestershire starting two days later, on July 23, at Maidstone.

This game, unfortunately, was ruined by rain but, now batting down another place at number eight, I remained 16 not out in the Kent first innings before bowling 10 overs for 23 runs. It was not world-beating stuff, of course, but I remember feeling pleased enough that I had contributed something. It was a start, too, and getting this precious chance of a start was everything that I desired at that age.

Imagine my frustration, then, that my cricket career was now - at such a crucial stage - about to be put on hold. In limbo, in fact, would be a better way of putting it. Just two days after the watery end of that match against Worcestershire at The Mote, I was catching a train to far-off Oswestry in Shropshire. Instead of serving Kent, which was all that I had ever wanted, I was off to serve Queen and country.

Chapter 4
National Service

Being called up for National Service almost cost me my professional cricket career. Then again, I suppose it did give me the chance to spend my 21st birthday doing guard duty at Shoeburyness, to qualify as a radio operator, to learn to drive 10-ton trucks, to score a century at Lord's, to represent Pembrokeshire, and to master the art of polishing your Army boots until you could see your face in them.

What is it about boots? They seemed to dominate my existence in those days. First, while on the Kent staff, I had cleaned enough of other people's boots to last me a lifetime. Now, in the Royal Artillery as 23581413 Gunner Luckhurst, it was the condition of my own footwear which assumed huge importance.

I've still got my Army boots, too, and I keep them in my garage. I even paid 50p (or 10 shillings as it was then) for the privilege of hanging on to them when my two years of National Service ended. Why not? I polished the bloody things so often, and for so long, that I thought they would be the perfect keepsake. It would have been such a waste of all that effort just to throw them away!

When I received my call-up papers, a month or so before my train journey up to Oswestry to enlist, I was asked for my preference: Army, Navy or Air Force? Because I was interested in planes, I ticked the box for the RAF. When I heard I had been posted to join the Royal Artillery, I wondered why they had bothered to ask.

I was part of an intake of approximately 200. We all queued up, and were issued with our equipment and clothing: trousers, tunic, socks… and boots. We then had to hand in a card, on which we told them what job we had done out on Civvy Street. I had written 'professional cricketer' - and within hours I received a message telling me I was required to represent the regiment's cricket team for two one-day matches being played on that coming weekend!

A result? Don't be fooled. Instead of having a weekend free to get myself properly prepared for initial inspection on the Monday morning, along with all the other new boys, I had to stay up to the early hours of the morning on both that Saturday and Sunday night in order to get all my kit neatly 'squared off', and to get those boots polished up for the first time.

To burn off the leather pimples that appeared on the toecap of your new boots, you had to heat up the flat side of a spoon in a candle flame and then work the spoon around the toe of the boots until the spots were burnt off and the leather was flat. Then it was a case of applying the polish with a wet cloth duster, and polishing it all up with a dry one. After several coats of black polish you had got boots shining like a mirror and, of course, your life would be hell if they weren't.

Only those who have also been in the Army will know just how much time all this polishing and shining takes. Was it all necessary? Well, it certainly helped to instil discipline - as did so many other aspects of Army life. Looking back, I think National Service did me a lot of good as a person. There is no doubt about that. But, at the time, I could have done with it coming along a year or so later, because to be yanked out of county cricket just 10 days after my first-class debut - and after just three first-class appearances - was cruel.

CARDIGANSHIRE 75
PEMBROKESHIRE 77—4

The bowling of Burton veteran Howard Goodridge set Pembroke on the way to victory over Cardiganshire at Lampeter on Wednesday. In a spell which included 4 maidens he took 6 for 7.

Cardigan were all out for 75.

Pembrokeshire started badly. Banner and Morris failing to score. The later batsmen took command, enabling Pembrokeshire to win by six wickets. Luckhurst carried his bat for 33, which included five fours.

Cardiganshire:—

D. H. Davies lbw H. Goodridge 15
A. Phillips lbw Evans 7
N. A. Maclean c Holly b Morris 22
J. R. Jones c Thomas b Morris 10
P. Craig b Goodridge 6
P. Ramsey lbw Goodridge 0
D. H. Jones lbw Goodridge 2
R. James c Banner b Goodridge 1
D. Griffiths c Luckhurst b Thomas...... 6
J. E. Tulley not out 4
T. Harries b Goodridge 0
Extras 2

Total 75

Bowling: J. Evans 1 for 13; D. Morris 2 for 21; H. Goodridge 6 for 7; J. R. Thomas 1 for 7.

Pembrokeshire:—

G. Banner c Jones b Ramsey 0
D. Morris b Tulley... 0
M. Cole lbw Ramsey 8
D. Hayward b Tulley 15
B. Luckhurst not out 33
G. Thomas not out... 15
Extras 6

Total for 4 wkts....... 77

T. Kiff, H. Goodridge, R. Holly, J. Evans and J. R. Thomas (capt.) did not bat.

Bowling: J. E. Tulley 2 for 39; P. Ramsey 2 for 32.

Match Drawn
LORD'S GROUND 4D

ROYAL ARTILLERY v. ROYAL ENGINEERS
Monday & Tuesday, July 6, 7, 1959 (2-day Match)

ROYAL ENGINEERS	First Innings		Second Innings	
†1 Maj. H. E. H. Newman	c Biggs b Stepto	7	c and b Luckhurst	25
2 Capt. W. N. J. Withall	c and b Luckhurst	65	c Biggs b Grace	67
3 2/Lt. R. L. Peck	not out	100	st Biggs b Grace	30
4 2/Lt. P. G. Hatch	c and b Luckhurst	0	st Biggs b Luckhurst	13
5 W.O.I R. P. Frost	l b w b Luckhurst	0	st Biggs b Jarmain	27
6 S/Sgt. S. Collett	c Biggs b Jarmain	53	l b w b Gardner	0
*7 Cpl. T. Surgett	not out	8	not out	8
8 Lt. M. A. Bromage			not out	7
9 Cpt. G. N. Tomlinson	Innings closed		Innings closed	
10 L/Cpl. R. Carter				
11 L/Cpl. M. D. Johnson				
	B 5 l-b , w , n-b	5	B 3, l-b 7, w , n-b	10
	Total	238	Total	187

FALL OF THE WICKETS

1—7 2—115 3—119 4—119 5—229 6— 7— 8— 9— 10—
1—81 2—105 3—126 4—162 5—163 6—180 7— 8— 9— 10—

ANALYSIS OF BOWLING

Name	1st Innings						2nd Innings					
	O.	M.	R.	W.	Wd.	N-b	O.	M.	R.	W.	Wd.	N-b
Salmon	12	3	45	0		...	3	0	11	0		...
Stepto	15	5	32	1		...	6	2	18	0		...
Gardner	5	2	13	0		...	8	2	24	1		...
Grace	23	6	68	0		...	21.2	3	70	2		...
Luckhurst	15	8	24	3		...	17	3	38	2		...
Jarmain	17	2	61	1		...	2	0	3	1		...
Wilkins							7	3	13	0		...

ROYAL ARTILLERY	First Innings		Second Innings	
1 Maj. R. D. Hawkes	b Johnson	42	c Peck b Johnson	1
2 2/Lt. M. A. Wilkins	b Tomlinson	47	c Peck b Tomlinson	10
3 Gnr. B. W. Luckhurst	not out	100	c Peck b Tomlinson	1
4 Capt. J. R. Tozer	l b w b Collett	17	c Peck b Tomlinson	25
5 Capt. W. T. Selley	not out	26	c Surgett b Tomlinson	13
6 Sgt. D. R. Salmon			c Tomlinson b Carter	65
*7 Maj. H. B. C. Gardner			c Carter b Tomlinson	6
8 Maj. G. F. Grace	Innings closed		not out	39
9 Capt. D. T. Jarmain			c Tomlinson b Carter	3
*10 Maj. I. E. G. Biggs			l b w b Johnson	3
11 Capt. A. S. Stepto			not out	1
	B , l-b 5, w , n-b	5	B 6, l-b 5, w , n-b	11
	Total	237	Total	178

FALL OF THE WICKETS

1—48 2—121 3—144 4— 5— 6— 7— 8— 9— 10—
1—35 2—38 3—38 4—76 5—98 6—151 7—163 8—164 9—176 10—

ANALYSIS OF BOWLING

Name	1st Innings						2nd Innings					
	O.	M.	R.	W.	Wd.	N-b	O.	M.	R.	W.	Wd.	N-b
Johnson	20	4	79	1		...	17	3	65	2		...
Bromage	17	2	61	0		...	9	1	39	1		...
Carter	7	0	33	0		...	3	0	16	2		...
Tomlinson	15	2	47	1		...	13	0	47	4		...
Collett	2	0	12	1		...						

Umpires—W. B. Morris & A. E. Bradford Scorers—Mrs. M. Wright & C. Fookes
† Captain * Wicket-keeper
Play begins at 11 each day Stumps drawn at 6.30 each day
Spectators are requested not to enter or leave their seats during the progress of an over

Royal Engineers won the toss

The scorecard which tells the story of my first hundred at Lord's

The reality, though, was that I was in the Army and that I had to get on with it. Initially, after the early settling-in period, that reality meant for me a 14-week training course in Rhyl, North Wales, to learn to become a radio operator.

From the camp in Rhyl, you used to get taken up to a lot of the nearby farms so that you could practice contacting each other over the radios. At the end of my course, I suddenly found myself being employed as one of the drivers who had to take the new intake of fledgling radio operators up to the various farms in a one-ton Army truck.

Looking back, I would have liked to have been posted to Cyprus, or somewhere a little bit more exotic and interesting, but there I was in the winter of 1958-59 driving people around the farmland of North Wales!

As the 1959 summer approached, however, it was realised at Royal Artillery headquarters in Woolwich that Gunner Luckhurst could be more gainfully utilised - as a cricketer - if he was stationed a little bit closer to base. That way, my seniors reasoned, I could be drafted in to the Royal Artillery first XI every weekend to do my bit for the honour of the regiment.

Accordingly, I soon found myself transferred from Rhyl to Gravesend and, most weekends, I had to catch a bus to Woolwich to play in matches against other Army teams or wandering clubs like I Zingari and the Band of Brothers. There were 10 officers and myself in the Artillery team, and in one match I very clearly remember an opposing batsman top-edging an attempted pull straight up into the air. "Yours, captain" came a shout… and seven of our fielders collided trying to make the catch!

After play had finished, however, all 10 of my teammates used to retire to the Officer's Mess. But as one of the lower ranks I, of course, was not allowed to join them. Instead, most Saturday nights that summer, I used to go home on the bus to Sittingbourne.

It was slightly surreal, being in the Army but also being able to go home for one night most weeks, and being stationed in Kent but feeling as if my previous life as a Kent professional cricketer based down the road at Canterbury was a million miles away.

I was very fortunate, however, that the Royal Artillery HQ was in Woolwich, and that I was able to get the chance to call in at home so often. What if it had been up in the north of Scotland, or somewhere equally distant?

At least, too, in the summer months, I was being given the opportunity to play a lot of cricket. As I was to realise later, it was not of a standard to do me much good in terms of my overall development, but it was enjoyable enough at the time. I also quickly earned selection for the composite Army XI, which enabled me to play in some more demanding fixtures, but the biggest match of every season was the Royal Artillery versus the Royal Engineers at Lord's.

My appearance in the 1959 fixture brought me a double pleasure: my very first game at Lord's, a ground which was to play such a central role in my subsequent career, and also my first century at the game's headquarters. In general terms, I suppose my time in the Army did enable me to gain more confidence as a batsman, simply due to crease occupation if nothing else, but I remember that spin bowling was much harder work on our home ground at Woolwich, which always boasted a very flat pitch!

The game at Lord's also has an interesting footnote. One of my opponents that day was Richard Peck, then a second lieutenant, but when I met him 20 years later he was a colonel. I had taken a Kent second XI team to play a match against an Army side at Aldershot, and afterwards we were all invited into the Officer's Mess for drinks and something to eat (how times change!). Suddenly, an officer came up to me and introduced himself as my former fellow cricketer at Lord's in 1959. In fact, he had also made a hundred in the match. It was wonderful to meet him and, later, I heard that he had been promoted again to become General Peck. We had been just two young lads playing cricket together in 1959 - but I had gone on to play for England and he eventually became a general!

When I was transferred to Gravesend I had been told to continue in my north Wales role of being a driver. But I also went on a course which instructed me in the art of driving a 10-ton lorry, and on one unforgettable occasion about eight of us landed up watching an England football international at Wembley! Our instructor was a fanatical football man, and so he decided that our 'training' would be to drive all the way to north London and then back to Gravesend. We stopped for just enough time to catch the match, of course!

Some of my other driving experiences were not quite so memorable, however. Once, I was fined for wasting Army time after calling out a sergeant in the belief that my lorry had broken down. I had just started a return journey to Gravesend, from Shornecliffe near Folkestone, when the vehicle spluttered to a stop. What I had not realised, despite my so-called training, was that the one-ton lorry I was driving had two separate fuel tanks. I knew I had to flick a switch down, when one was empty, but I was ignorant of the fact that I also had to turn over the fuel lines. The sergeant who I had telephoned, in a fluster, was none too pleased to discover my error when he finally arrived at the half-way point of his 120-mile mercy trip... especially as he had been about to start a 72-hour period of leave!

There was also the time I was detailed to join a convoy taking gunnery equipment all the way from Gravesend to Tenby in west Wales. That was quite a journey in those pre-motorway days, I can tell you, and even more daunting when you never go above 20 miles per hour. We spent all day packing up the lorries, and then set off to drive through the night. One night would only take us part of the way, of course, but we could then stop for rest the following day and continue on when darkness fell again, in order not to disrupt the daytime traffic.

There must have been about 30 vehicles in this convoy, and I was stuck somewhere in the middle of them. By the time that we reached the Staines by-pass, on that first night, my eyes were going. The colleague in the passenger's seat, whose job it was to make sure I did not doze off, was fast asleep - and all I had to focus on was the two red tail-lights of the lorry directly in front of me. At a pedestrian 20 mph, it was difficult after a while to do anything other than nod off - and that's what I did. The convoy went on, but I mounted the pavement on the near side and ran into a lamp-post. I only clipped it, in fact, because the jolt of hitting the curb had woken me from my slumber and I had managed to swerve away from it. A passing police car, nevertheless, had witnessed this incident, and I soon had the long arm of the law on my shoulder. At 20, I was also still a touch naive, and when the policeman asked me what had happened, I replied: "I fell asleep, sir". The policeman then said: "But what about that cat which ran across the road in front of you?" Still not catching on, I said: "What cat?" No doubt, by this time, raising his eyes, the kindly copper answered: "The cat you swerved to avoid, of course!" By now, thankfully, I realised what was going on and I thanked the policeman profusely. He wrote out a statement, detailing the cat incident, and when - on my eventual return to Gravesend six weeks later - I was called up to answer the automatic charge for 'crashing' an Army vehicle, it was his statement which got me off. The case was dismissed, but not that my battery commander was hoodwinked. "I understand, Luckhurst, that you have had some trouble with sleeping cats!" he greeted me, with a smirk, on my return.

The other good things which came out of that seemingly endless journey to Tenby in the summer of '59 was the chance to spend a virtual six-week holiday at the resort, waiting there while the guns were tested out to sea, and the sudden, unexpected opportunity to represent Pembrokeshire.

While we were lounging around the place one day a message came through to the office asking if there were any decent cricketers amongst us Army types. Apparently,

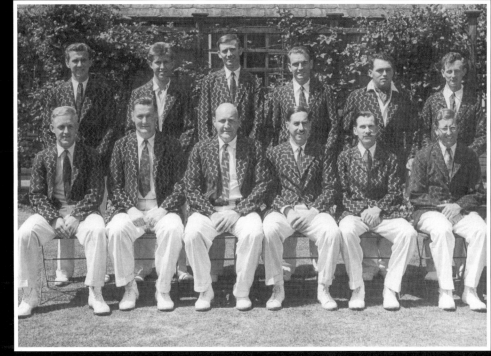

The Royal Artillery team, pictured before the 1959 fixture against the Royal Engineers at Lord's. The XI is made up of nine officers, one sergeant and one lowly gunner... me!

A three-in-one picture: I am wearing the tie given to me by Bill Fairservice, holding my old Army boots, and behind me is one of the wheels from the old St Lawrence Ground scorebox which I used to turn as a young professional

Pembrokeshire were playing a minor county match the following day and they were two men short. Myself and another lad were duly volunteered for action, and off I went! I ended up playing two matches for them, though I must confess I couldn't recall much about them when I was recently very kindly sent the details of the games!

I was given a Pembrokeshire tie to commemorate my debut, however, which I was proudly able to wear when I was invited, equally out of the blue, to an official county dinner hosted by the club 10 years ago. This time, I enjoyed a very pleasant journey from my home near Dover to west Wales, and a very convivial evening as my wife and I found ourselves sitting next to another ex-Pembrokeshire player Alan Jones, the former Glamorgan opener who I also opened the England batting alongside when he and I made our international debuts against the Rest of the World in 1970. So, when you next see me described as 'Brian Luckhurst, formerly of Kent and England' you will know that it is actually an incorrect epithet. It should be, in fact, 'Brian Luckhurst, formerly of Kent, Pembrokeshire and England'!

In the 1960 summer, before I was demobbed in late July, I played both for the Army team and the Combined Services, but by then I was no longer stationed at Gravesend. That camp, which housed the last heavy ack-ack (anti-aircraft) regiment the Army had, was closed down at the end of 1959. Guided weapons were now the thing, and 80 per cent of my regiment were sent to do duty at one of those camps in the Outer Hebrides. Again, because of my usefulness as a cricketer, I was spared that dubious honour. Instead, I was posted to Shoeburyness in Essex - so that I was still in hailing distance of Woolwich.

That was how, in February 1960, I found myself amongst a small band of other soldiers on guard duty on the evening of my 21st birthday. We were guarding millions and millions of pounds worth of guided weapons… with pick-axe handles! Even now, I can vividly remember gazing out across the Thames Estuary to Kent, and seeing the bright lights of Sheerness shining out in the darkness.

At Shoeburyness, indeed, I became used to doing night guard duty. My sergeant-major there was of the opinion that playing cricket equalled skiving, and during my final summer in the Army I found myself on the night-time rota every time I arrived back at camp following a game!

So, although I had trained to be a radio operator, I never actually got to do that particular job during my Army career. I drove trucks, did guard duty, played cricket, and polished up my boots. Most of all, I learned the truth of the old Army saying: "If it moves, salute it. If it doesn't, paint it". Keeping your nose clean, and your head down, is a big part of Army life - but, at the same time, I think my experiences in those two years did a lot to toughen me up and, indeed, help me to grow up.

Yes, I had got used in the preceding four years to doing the chores expected of a young cricket professional, but the Army was still a far different world. As I've said before, I was very much a spoilt brat in my early teens, and I think National Service did me the power of good.

I learned far more about discipline, and self-discipline, and it gave me more of an understanding of other people. It taught me to respect other people, and to respect rank. If you were told to do something, you did it. There were no questions.

Yet if it improved me and made me more rounded as a person, my National Service years were also harmful for my cricket. I had played a lot of cricket in my time in the Army, but sadly it had not advanced me as a cricketer. At best I had stagnated, and in many respects I had gone backwards.

When, at the end of July 1958, I boarded that train for Oswestry, I had done so as a true first-class cricketer. Now, two years later, as I left Shoeburyness and the Army behind, I knew that the next chapter of my life's journey was going to bring the very difficult business of trying to make up for lost time.

Chapter 5
The Swinging Sixties

If the 1950's shaped me as a cricketer and as a person, then it was the 1960's that made me. By the end of that decade of great social change I was an established county player, and even being talked about as an England possible. Yes, the Sixties were swinging around me, all right, but in my own little world it was all about fulfilling my dream. Moreover, if it wasn't for Colin Page back in 1961, I'm not sure I would have had a dream left to fulfil.

My personal life had changed significantly in September 1960, too, at the end of a summer which started with me in the Army and ended with me back in the Kent second team, because I had got married. That brought with it, of course, an added responsibility for a 21-year old with hardly any money and what seemed to be few prospects - of any certain nature, anyway.

I had my basic winter retainer from Kent for that 1960-61 close season, but I also needed a job to see me through to the following April. Using my Sittingbourne 'connections', I managed to get employment with furniture store J Peters and Sons, a firm which might be described as being the town's equivalent of Harvey Nichols, doing furniture removals.

After our wedding on September 3, my wife Elaine and I went to live with my mother and father. There was no bathroom at our family house at 69 Canterbury Road, and just an outside toilet, but my new wife and I had no money to speak of and could not afford to put down a deposit for a house of our own. For six months after our marriage, therefore, we had to depend on my parents for a roof over our heads.

Things only changed after a chance conversation with Doug Bowyer, then the landlord of the Rose and Crown pub in Sittingbourne High Street. On occasions, I used to go there for a drink or two after work, and one day I told Doug that I was looking for somewhere to live locally. He told me to go to speak to the manager of the Lloyds Bank branch next to the pub, saying he had heard that there were a couple of flats available for rent in the building.

Tommy Atkins was the bank manager, and when I knocked on his door he was initially unforthcoming. "I think that they have both been taken," he told me. I then mentioned who I was, and that I was fairly recently married and looking for a place that we could call our own. I don't know whether it was the words "Kent cricketer" that did the trick (I suspect that it was!) but Mr Atkins then said: "On second thoughts, I think I might have one of the flats available".

My wife and I moved in soon afterwards and, for the next few years, our home was one of those two one-bedroomed flats up above the bank manager's own flat. And, when we finally found ourselves in a position to be able to actually buy a house, it was Mr Atkins who arranged the finances for us to purchase one of the new two-bedroomed houses that were then being built at Milton Regis. I remember it cost us £1,995, but my salary at the time was only about £600 per year and I needed Mr Atkins to convince me that I could afford to buy it!

At the start of the 1961 season, though, I had a wife to support and the rent to pay on the first place of our own, but most importantly of all I was a 22-year old professional cricketer who had played three first-class matches back in 1958 but - cricket-wise - had done almost nothing of note since.

In 11 innings for the second XI at the end of the 1960 summer I had scored 230 runs at an average of 25.55, with one half-century, and had picked up 14 wickets at 16.21. In the whole of the 1961 season, though, my second XI figures were conspicuously worse. From 20 innings I managed just 298 runs at 21.28, with a top score of only 46, while my 35 wickets came at a cost of 26.62 runs apiece. I couldn't even make a fifty in any of my nine innings for the Club and Ground side.

It was a depressing summer for me, and as it drew to an end I did not expect to be retained. I was bitterly disappointed that I did not seem to have made any progress as a cricketer, and I had also been around the game for long enough by then to realise the harsh realities of professional sporting life.

I still wanted it as badly as ever, but success depends on getting results and mine were simply not good enough. There were also others around at the club who, by now, had made the sort of progress that I was seeking - batsmen like John Prodger and David Constant, who in that 1961 second XI season scored 775 and 1075 runs respectively at averages well into the 40's. Also, in my first five years at the club, I had witnessed the then rapid turnover of young professionals - with no fewer than 20 being told they were not being retained during that time. So, now, was it my turn?

Perhaps the main reason I thought my career was over, however, was the fact that, since my first team debut three years earlier, there were others who had come through the system. Playing his first games for the second XI that 1961 summer, for instance, was a certain Mike Denness - who averaged 55 from six innings after leaving the west of Scotland for the sunnier climes of the Garden of England!

Yet, although I was so downbeat about my own lack of progress, I soon discovered that there was one man at Kent who still believed in me. Colin Page, the second XI coach, took me to one side and suggested that it might take more than one summer for me to get back to where I had been before my National Service began. Besides, he said, I was not the only cricketer he had seen struggle to readjust after two years out of the game.

I am sure that Colin put in a strong word on my behalf with the Kent committee at the end of that summer, and I am just so pleased that I was able to repay his trust. Colin Page saved my career and, 10 months later, he was also the man who gave me my precious chance of a first team recall.

I was massively relieved to be given another year's contract for 1962, but I knew that this time it really was make or break. I was 23, it was eight years since I joined the staff and I was clinging on to my job as a professional cricketer, if not yet by my fingertips then at least by my fingers. Having started out so young, moreover, I had no other qualifications (other than to drive lorries!) and so I began that summer even more determined - if that were possible - to hold on to what I had got.

Pre-season preparation in that era was still rudimentary, and after eight weeks of Tuesday evening nets at the indoor cricket school at Gillingham - which was then the only facility of sufficient standard in Kent - we had a fortnight of training at the University of Kent and then four weeks of outdoor nets at the St Lawrence Ground. Before that 1962 season, I would have done a lot of bowling and fielding (as a fetcher of balls hit out of the nets, mainly) but no batting practice in the nets. Only the first XI batsmen were given that honour!

But what must be stressed here is that even at that age and at that stage of my career I was still regarded mainly as a bowler, anyway. True, my batting had developed to the extent that I was seen as a lower-order all-rounder, but if I was going to win selection for the first team again it would be more because of my spin-bowling ability.

Fred Trueman saying sorry to me after breaking one of my fingers in the 1967 fixture against Yorkshire at Canterbury

Talking to one of the greats… Kent's own Frank Woolley

The Kent team is introduced to the Duchess of Kent by Colin Cowdrey. A young Derek Underwood
s centre of attention

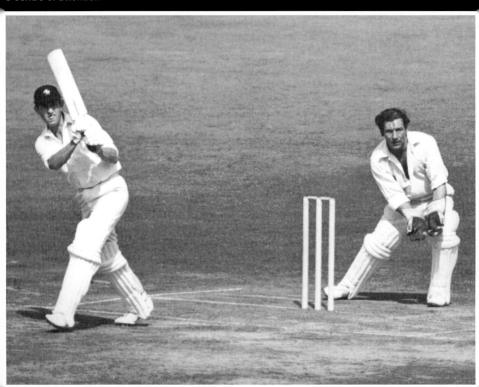

t looks a good shot, but this clip off my pads brought my downfall for 54 in the 1967 Gillette Cup fina

It was a good job, really. On May 24 and 25, in a second XI fixture at Northampton, I bagged a pair! Imagine how I felt as I trudged off the field with a second nought to my name - and, looking back now, I can still feel some of my sense of despair. Imagine, however, how I then felt at the end of the match when Colin Page informed me that I would be playing for the first team the following week!

Colin had just received a call from Les Ames, who was in charge of first team affairs, asking him to recommend two players for promotion for the championship fixture against Somerset at Gravesend, starting on May 30.

Kent had made a poor start to the championship season, losing two and drawing four of their first six matches, and Colin Cowdrey was about to depart to play for England in the first Test of the summer. Alan Dixon and Alan Brown were also out injured and, as it transpired, David Nicholls and David 'Doughie' Baker were eventually brought into the team as well as myself.

But, most vitally for me, Colin Page had given my name to Les as one of the two he felt were ready for first team action. He could not have told Les about the two noughts, though, and I still wonder to this day what Les subsequently thought about my promotion when he heard about it!

For me, this was deep breath time. I knew it was now or never. Going into that Somerset game, I knew that the next three days would go a long way to deciding whether I had it in me to be a fully-fledged professional. Colin Page had taken a big chance on me - what else could it have been on the back of a pair? But he clearly still believed, against much of the hard evidence, that I had what it took. And at least, however, it was now down to me. Despite everything, this was the opportunity I had been living for.

The game began with Somerset batting first, and I took 4-32 from 11 overs. It was the start I needed, and given that bowling was my supposed major suit in those days it should not be so surprising to look back on it now. But the fact remains - and this has tickled me in all the years since - that it was an analysis which remained the best bowling figures of my entire first-class career! Given how I then developed as a batsman, and given that inside 12 months a rather better left-arm spinner than me had emerged at Kent - a young chap called Underwood - it is amazing to think that it was a bowling spell that was so important to me.

Anyway, I took another wicket in Somerset's second innings and scored 17 in our first innings, but we were then 104-5 and sinking fast in our own second innings when I came out to bat - again at number seven - at 3.19pm on the final afternoon. Brian Langford and Ken Palmer were doing the damage on a wearing pitch, but Peter Richardson was still there for us and my job was to hang on with him. With the confidence of my wickets to bolster me, I did hang on.

Richardson finally made 135, and I ended up 71 not out when the match was drawn. We had put on 116 for the sixth wicket and I went on to bat for two and three-quarter hours to help to save the game. As I walked off at the end, I knew I was on my way at last.

The very next day saw us starting another match, against Warwickshire at Folkestone, and I made 37 and 10 not out (again from number seven) as we won by 12 runs in seamer-friendly conditions that limited my bowling opportunity to just seven wicket-less overs.

Elevated to number six in the order for the next game, away against Essex at Romford from June 6-8, I scored 33 and 22. Then left out of the away trip to Hampshire, I was recalled for Tunbridge Wells week and made 51 from number six against Worcestershire before being pushed up again to five for the Sussex match, in which I scored 0 and 42.

From there, I was a fixture in the side for the rest of the season. Further highlights were 72 against Yorkshire at Gillingham in mid-August and an unbeaten 86 at Bristol in late August which took me past the coveted 1000 runs for the season. That innings against Gloucestershire was a double joy for me, because I helped Colin Cowdrey to put on an unbroken 233 for the fourth wicket. Colin got 148 not out and to be batting at the other end was always such an education!

An unbeaten 72 against Middlesex at Lord's in the final match, in early September, meant I had totalled 1096 runs for the season at an average of 35.53. I had played 22 championship matches and, by now, it did not matter that my paltry tally of 13 wickets had cost 42 runs each. I had proved myself as a batsman, and as a county cricketer, and I was holding down a regular position at number five. And all on the back of that pair at Northampton!

In 1963 I alternated between the middle-order and opener, with my first outing as an opening batsman coming from May 8-10 in the match against Yorkshire at Hull. Fred Trueman was one of the new ball bowlers in a rain-affected draw, but the match is significant in Kent history because it also saw the first-class debut of Derek Underwood. Then 17, 'Deadly' took 4-40 from 21 overs in Yorkshire's first innings on his way to 101 wickets at 21.12 in a remarkable debut season. Mike Denness was batting at number five in that match, too, and I suppose you could say that this was the game which marked a tangible beginning to the growth of a team destined to become Kent's best.

I was back down the order however, at number six, when I scored my maiden first-class hundred in late July. The week after that unbeaten 126, against Surrey at Blackheath, I was presented with my county cap. It was during Canterbury Week, and I went off to buy the team a dozen bottles of champagne, as was the tradition. It was a sweet moment indeed to share a celebration drink with my teammates in the same dressing room where I had cleaned all those boots so many years before.

My 30 first-class matches in 1963 brought me 1501 runs at 33.35, and Derek Underwood's arrival meant I hardly got a bowl. Indeed, my three wickets cost more than 100 runs apiece! I also topped the catches list, with 23, and this side of my game was to become very important as my career went on.

In the Kent second XI that summer, meanwhile, appeared one A P E Knott and one A G E Ealham. The 18-year old Alan Ealham only played six innings, but a 17-year old Knotty - then an off-spinning all-rounder would you believe - batted 25 times and also bowled a total of 35 overs! By 1964, however, Knott was keeping wicket and that summer played 10 matches as first XI keeper. In 1965, he was the regular wicket-keeper in succession to Derek Ufton and Tony Catt and - with Derek Underwood - was on the verge of becoming one of both Kent and England's classiest and best-known double acts.

It is fascinating to look back and chart how the great Kent team of the 1970's gradually built up during the 1960's. I established myself in 1962, and both Denness and Underwood became fixtures in 1963. Knott arrived on the scene in 1964 and both Norman Graham and John Shepherd joined the staff in 1965, before making their first team debuts the following summer. By 1966, too, Ealham was a first team regular and all the while, of course, we had the guidance of Colin Cowdrey as captain. Colin had been appointed skipper in 1957 and was to remain in the post until the 1971 season.

It was during the 1965 season that Peter Richardson left the club, leaving the Luckhurst-Denness opening partnership to succeed the Richardson-Luckhurst alliance. By then it was pretty obvious to everybody that Underwood and Knott were going to be pretty special cricketers, and Mike and I had also developed a great friendship as well as a great understanding out in the middle.

L. E. G. AMES (Secretary/Manager)   J. N. SHEPHERD   A. BROWN   J. N. GRAHAM   D. L. UNDERWOOD   A. EALHAM   A. P. KNOTT

The Kent team which beat Sussex in the 1967 Gillette Cup semi-final at Canterbury

The Kent team walks out at Hastings in 1967. From left to right: John Shepherd, Mike Denness, Alan Brown, Stuart Leary, Norman Graham, Colin Cowdrey, Derek Underwood, myself, Alan Dixon, Bob Wilson, Alan Knott

Senior players like Stuart Leary, Bob Wilson, Alan Dixon and Alan Brown were also very much to the fore in the middle 1960's, and it is a sadness to me that Wilson did not quite make it to play in our first trophy-winning side in 1967.

Like me, Bob was a Sittingbourne man, born and bred, and indeed he was my first opening partner for Kent up there in Hull in May 1963. He scored almost 20,000 first-class runs for Kent, with 30 hundreds, and if he had been born five years later he would have experienced all the thrills of winning things that I was fortunate enough to have. I always think that Neil Taylor and Mark Benson, from a later generation, also fall into that category of cricketer unlucky to come along when they did.

Actually, Bob was in the Kent team which won its first match of that successful 1967 Gillette Cup campaign, our breakthrough victory, but he then became sidelined and he retired soon after we lifted the trophy at Lord's that September.

As a team, we were definitely aware in the mid-60's that we were growing stronger, and in both 1967 and 1968 we came second in the championship to underline that growth. It was the Gillette Cup triumph of 1967, though, which ended a barren 54 years for the club, and which provided the inspiration for the glory years to follow.

Learning how to make it over the winning line is the greatest challenge of all in sport. There are always plenty of people and teams around with high promise, but winning is another matter. There are those, too, who manage to win once but then cannot quite bring it off again. True winners are those who do it again and again, but back in 1967 we were a team who just wanted to manage it that first time!

For the first four years of the Gillette Cup, which began in 1963, we had been knocked out in the first round each time. But, by the time we reached the 1967 semi-final, which was against Sussex at Canterbury, the pressure was on us to show we could be winners - not also-rans.

There were around 18,000 spectators packed into the St Lawrence Ground that day, on July 19, and when Mike Denness and I walked out to open the Kent innings you could have heard a pin drop. The tension around the ground was like nothing I had known before, and yet it was merely increased by a further few notches when I played and missed a couple of times at Tony Buss in the first over!

Handling the emotions and the pressures of those sort of occasions is what performing at the top level is all about. All your senses are heightened, but it can be an intimidating experience and you have to be able to deal with it.

That semi-final against Sussex was a huge game in the development of the great Kent side. We were aware of that, too, and that only added to the magnitude of it. That semi-final was, for that reason, a much tenser affair for us than the final itself - even though the margin of our victory against Sussex was so much bigger in the end than it was over Somerset at Lord's.

John Shepherd was pushed up to bat at three against Sussex, even though Mike was out early, and he and I added 135 for the second wicket. He got 77, and then Colin Cowdrey came in at number four with the score at 138-2 and proceeded to play one of the best innings I've ever seen. We added a further 67, before I was out for 78, but Colin went on to score 78 himself and in the process he took John Snow apart - which was a rarity in itself. Snow worked up a great pace, and tried all he knew, but his 11 overs still went for 65 runs, which must be one of the few times he ever conceded six an over in his career. Colin creamed Snowy around the St Lawrence Ground, and the atmosphere by then was simply electric. Eventually, we totalled 293-5 from our 60 overs, and Sussex could make only 175 in reply with both Brown and Underwood picking up three wickets at low cost.

There was now a six-week wait until the final, in which more excitement mounted in Kent.

As we were right in the championship battle, too, only losing out in the end to Yorkshire by 10 points as we finished runners-up, it all made for a thrilling end to the season.

Unfortunately for me, I missed the last three weeks of August after having a finger broken by Fred Trueman in the disappointing - and ultimately costly - defeat by Yorkshire at Canterbury. At least, however, I made it back for the Gillette Cup final on September 2, but it was touch and go that 24 days would prove to be long enough for the injury to heal. I wore a specially-made plaster cast which fitted over the back of my hand inside my glove, for added protection, but I was still in some discomfort as I dug in against the new ball after Colin had won the toss and chosen to bat.

Mike Denness made an elegant 50, in an opening stand of 78, and then Shepherd played well for 30 as we took the total to 138. Having made 54, however, which maintained my sequence of top-scoring for Kent in each round of that year's competition, I was caught off Bill Alley and inside an hour we were suddenly struggling at 150-7. Alan Knott and Alan Ealham steadied things again with a stand of 27, but an all out total of 193 meant we had to bowl and field well to prevent Somerset from stealing the prize away from us.

Although they reached 129-4 at one stage, we always felt in control and I had the added pleasure of taking two catches off Underwood's bowling as Somerset fell away to 161 all out. We had won by 32 runs and the sense of elation and relief, flooding through us in almost equal measure, carried on into our celebrations that evening.

It had been a wonderful occasion, with both the Somerset and Kent fans arriving laden with either cider-barrels or big bundles of hops, and many of the West Countrymen dressed up as country bumpkins with smocks and string tied around the knees of their trousers. But both sets of fans behaved superbly, and mingled good-naturedly as the cider and beer flowed. Afterwards, there were some lovely moments as players mingled with a throng of Kent fans gathering around the Grace Gates to greet those of us who had ventured out from the dressing room celebrations.

It was such a release after the tensions of the day although, as I say, they didn't seem to be as great as during the Canterbury semi-final. But there had still been apprehension before the start, especially as so many of us then had never before played in front of a full house at Lord's. I have never felt frightened before a match, even when the quickest bowlers in the world were playing for the opposition. But you always feel apprehensive, and I think most cricketers feel the fear of failing that I always had. My feelings at the end of that first Kent trophy win can best be summed up by the explanation of why I am not in a famous photograph taken of the team brandishing the Gillette Cup aloft in front of the Lord's pavilion soon after the game ended. The reason? I had dashed through the Long Room and up to our dressing room in order to get myself a well-earned beer!

A cup final day is a special time in the career of any cricketer, and who were we to know that this was going to be the first of many such experiences? When we walked into Lord's that morning we were merely a cricket team with a lot of potential. But when we walked out of that great ground we had proved that we were winners. It was an incredible day, full of the excitement of realising that we could be taking part in a new, long overdue era of success for Kent cricket.

Chapter 6
Champions

Kent's achievement in the club's centenary summer of 1970 must rank alongside any of the more remarkable stories which sport throws up with glorious regularity. To be bottom of the county championship table on July 1, but then to go on to be crowned champions in early September, is the stuff of legend. Appropriate, really, as the 1970 triumph heralded the true coming of age of a Kent team destined for legendary status.

The Gillette Cup win of 1967 had given early notice of our growing talents, as a unit as much as individuals, but then the seasons of 1968 and 1969 were both highly disappointing in their different ways. Mutterings, as a result, could be heard about whether we were actually capable of pushing on to greater glory.

In the 1968 championship we finished as runners-up to Yorkshire for the second year in succession, despite winning more games than any other county. This was the last summer of the 28-match championship, and we were beaten into second place by, in effect, the new bonus point system that was put into place for that season. Yorkshire finished 14 points ahead of us, despite winning a match less, because their tally of bonus points (46 for batting and 114 for bowling) was 24 more than we managed (41 and 95).

Glamorgan, in third, were another 19 points distant, but we knew at the end of that campaign that we were good enough to have won it. Asif Iqbal had joined us for that 1968 season, strengthening our batting in particular but also proving an instant hit with the Kent public and further enlivening the dressing-room with his spirit and personality. John Dye had by now emerged as a considerable force with the new ball, while Alan Dixon and Norman Graham were also top-class performers at this stage. David Sayer and Alan Brown were highly effective fast bowlers in reserve, while in the middle-order Alan Ealham was growing more influential and Stuart Leary only just missed his 1000 runs.

John Shepherd, now one of the best all-rounders in the game, missed three matches with injury but still topped 1000 runs and took 96 wickets. Mike Denness and I scored almost 3000 runs between us at the top of the order and Colin Cowdrey averaged more than 40. Knott and Underwood were England regulars, alongside Colin, and in the second XI were two fine young prospects - Bob Woolmer and Graham Johnson. The 20-year old Woolmer took the most wickets for the seconds and, during Maidstone Week, celebrated his senior debut by scoring an undefeated 50 against Essex. Johnson, then 21, topped the second XI batting averages and came second in the bowling list. And, don't forget, we also had David Nicholls to keep wicket and biff runs when Knott was away on Test duty.

Crowds had also improved hugely as we improved our standing within the county game. In 1967 attendances around Kent were double those of 1966, and only the predominantly wet weather of 1968 prevented that graph from carrying on upwards. As it was, 12,000 came to the first day of the championship fixture against Yorkshire at Canterbury.

But people came because we were an exciting and, overall, a young side. We had strokemakers, great bowlers, a great wicket-keeper, and we were also tremendous to watch in the field. Asif, Shepherd, Dixon, Ealham and Denness were all world-class fielders. Colin Cowdrey was then still a world-class slip and I wasn't too shabby in the field either! We were, in short, a team that people felt was going places. And fans, as much and in some cases possibly more so than players, have their dreams. What a journey we were all about to go on, too... but not yet for a while.

The 1969 season was, frankly, forgettable. It was a big let-down for all concerned but there were good reasons for it. I enjoyed my best-ever summer in terms of first-class runs scored - 1914 at an average of 47.85 - and finished sixth in the national averages. I came close to England selection, only for Mike Denness to get the nod ahead of me during the series against New Zealand, but it was a combination of many other Test calls and a lengthy injury list which resulted in our eventual 10th place in the championship and fourth position in the newly-launched Sunday League.

Colin Cowdrey, then still England captain, missed virtually the rest of the season after snapping an Achilles tendon during a Sunday match at Maidstone on May 25, and John Shepherd appeared in only the last two championship games after needing time to recover from a back injury sustained while playing for the West Indies on their early-summer tour. Alan Dixon, too, suffered from injury that season, and with both Knott and Underwood away for most of the time on England duty we simply failed to overcome the constant disruption.

Perhaps 1969 was a necessary part of the team's development however. Perhaps all the difficulties which that summer threw at us resulted in a final growth to full maturity. Whatever, a big part of the glory of 1970 was that the Kent team managed to do what it did when no fewer than five of us - Knott, Underwood, Cowdrey, Denness and myself - were regularly absent on international business. I suppose it simply underlines the truism that it is the strength of a squad which wins long haul competitions like the county championship, not the strength of a few leading individuals.

I want now to chart the team's progress from July 1, 1970, on a match-by-match basis. That's because this will reveal how much of a team triumph it was, as much as recording the details of an almost miraculous achievement. Also, even though the team went on to collect 11 titles in 12 seasons, it is the 1970 championship success which in my views tops the lot!

Mike Denness was captaining the side when the Kent team turned up at Harlow on July 1 to begin a match against Essex. At that stage, it was just a question of getting off the bottom of the championship table, and once again there were four of us missing due to England selection: Cowdrey, Knott, Underwood and myself. Mike led from the front with 167 not out, and with Alan Ealham hitting 88 we declared our first innings at 330-7. Shepherd then took 5-41 as Essex were bowled out for 179 and, following on, they could make only 127 with Graham picking up 6-67 and Dye 4-51. Victory by an innings and 24 runs brought 18 points, but any lift in morale was immediately negated by a 136-run defeat against Middlesex at Lord's, despite Bob Woolmer's nine wickets in the match, and then a deflating loss to Sussex at Canterbury in the third round of the Gillette Cup on July 8.

I hold myself to blame for that defeat, too, because I ran myself out for 48 going for a third run when it was down to me to win the game. I had allowed the team to slip behind the clock, as we chased Sussex's 199, because I wanted to get myself in and well-set for the final push. I was still confident I could pull it off when I

Above: One of my favourite photographs, and the one which Colin Cowdrey made sure was taken in September 1970. Members of the Kent squad, plus physiotherapist Len Kilby, manager Les Ames, coach Colin Page and scorer Claude Lewis pose for an historic picture on the morning after Kent became county champions for the first time in 57 years

Left: The Master at work. Colin Cowdrey is pictured batting against Australia

made my fatal error of judgement. It was particularly annoying to fail, because I knew what a win would have meant to the team at that time. Eventually, we were all out for 152 with 19 balls left unbowled.

We then had two days' break before Maidstone Week, which featured championship fixtures against Derbyshire and Hampshire. It was after the rain-affected draw against Derbyshire, on the late afternoon of July 14, that we held a team conference in The Mote dressing room. Behind a locked door, we sat down with Les Ames to discuss what we were not doing right and what we had to do to get ourselves back to being the sort of team we all knew we could be. It was a frank meeting, but also a constructive one, and we decided that our approach from then on was going to be one of concentrated attack. We were going to chase as many batting bonus points as possible, and we were going to play extremely positive cricket at all times. In 1970, you see, there was a batting point available for every 25 runs scored above 150 inside the first 85 overs of your first innings - and it was going to be our success at collecting up these batting points which was to play a big part in the drive to the title.

Boosted by this clear-the-air discussion, and with renewed focus, the team gained 20 points from the 49-run win against Hampshire which featured 106 and 51 from Graham Johnson, who was promoted to open in my absence with England, and aggressive knocks of 88 by Stuart Leary and 78 by Asif. Denness scored 84 in the second innings and the win was sealed on the final afternoon by Richard Elms, the left-arm seamer, taking a four-wicket haul in his debut match. Shepherd and Dixon also both took five wickets during this game.

Then came a toughed-out draw at Sheffield after Yorkshire bowled us out for 132 and piled up a big first innings lead thanks to centuries from Geoff Boycott and Phil Sharpe. Denness, with 96, and Ealham (85) led the resistance. With the Test quartet back for the visit to Hove on July 25-28, we thrashed Sussex by 10 wickets. Colin Cowdrey and I added 154, and Alan Brown came in at number nine to thump 52 in little more than half-an-hour to make sure of a fifth batting point. Shepherd took a first innings 5-45 and Brown a second innings five-wicket haul as Sussex were dismissed for 154 and 158.

Canterbury Week, however, brought only two frustrating draws. A mere one point was taken from the August 1-4 match against Worcestershire in which Tom Graveney scored 114 in his farewell appearance in Kent, while Middlesex held out on 319-7 despite being tempted to go for their target of 356 in five and a half hours by our esteemed captain, Cowdrey, who gave himself 10 overs of his rarely-sighted leg-breaks and took a wicket - and who also asked me to send down three rather less successful overs! John Shepherd's 6-33, well supported by Derek Underwood, had given us early command as Middlesex were bowled out for a first innings 95 - 112 runs adrift - and then Cowdrey (84 not out) and Asif (88) had put on 140 in less than two hours before our second innings declaration at 243-4. But not even Underwood's 5-86 from 37.2 overs could prevent Peter Parfitt (83) and John Murray (97) from saving the game.

Our gallop up the table, in fact, only really began in earnest in the back-to-back wins against Somerset at Weston-super-Mare on August 8-11 and Gloucestershire at Cheltenham on August 15-18. Victory in Somerset was by the comfortable margin of 10 wickets, with Mike Denness' first innings 122 ensuring four batting points and a useful lead after Bob Woolmer's 6-53 had held the home side to 211. The Somerset second innings was sent spinning to 121 all out as Underwood (5-40) and Johnson (4-31) got to work, and Mike and I knocked off the 70 needed to win with little bother. It was the one wicket triumph over Gloucestershire at Cheltenham, though, which enabled the team to maintain a powerful momentum and instil yet more self-belief into the ranks. Underwood took 11 wickets in the match, as Gloucestershire were bowled out for 289 and 190. The only problem was that we had been dismissed ourselves for a first innings 140, with off-spinner John Mortimore taking 5-43 on a pitch giving the slower bowlers great assistance. Requiring 340 to win, no-one gave Kent a chance when the chase began on the second evening. I did not witness this match, being away again with England, but by all accounts both Mike Denness and Asif Iqbal batted with supreme skill in testing conditions to make 97 and 109 respectively. David Nicholls, deputising once more for Knott, struck 34 but four wickets then tumbled for nine runs when the winning post had been just 11 runs away. With two more runs required, last man Norman Graham joined Stuart Leary and a priceless single from each man took us gratefully over the line.

It was an incredible result, but even more drama was to come. After the next game at Northampton was abandoned as a rain-hit draw, we won victories at Blackheath and Folkestone that could hardly have been more thrilling. First, against Surrey on August 22-24 came a nail-biting 12-run success and then, against Nottinghamshire and Garry Sobers from August 29 to September 1, came a three-wicket triumph achieved with just eight balls to spare. At Blackheath it was Graham Johnson who was the star performer, taking 6-35 and then 6-116 with his much underrated off-spin after Colin Cowdrey had declared for the second time in the game to give Surrey the chance of a last afternoon run chase. In the end, set 263 to win, they fell just short when Pat Pocock tried to hit a six in the penultimate over - bowled by Johnson - and Asif took a wonderful running catch at long-off.

At Folkestone, I am proud to say it was me who played the innings that kept Kent's championship hopes bubbling. A scintillating first day 123 not out by Sobers had swept Notts to 376-4 declared, and early on the second day we found ourselves rocking badly at 27-5 in reply. Alan Ealham, however, joined me and put together an innings of 57 which clinched him his county cap. I don't think I ever played a more important innings for my county than the 156 not out I made that day, and the efforts of Alan and I earned a vital five batting points and also allowed Colin to make a declaration at 310-7 which challenged Notts to set us a target. This they did, although 282 in three hours was a stiff task. Mike Denness and I put on 103 for the first wicket in good time, and when I fell for 58 Mike went on to a brilliant 90. Asif then raced to 56 but, with three overs left, we still had a bit to do at 269-7. Alan Knott, however, is one of the best players any county team can have had coming in to bat in the lower order, and he hit three of the four balls he faced to the boundary to speed us home. We were ecstatic in the dressing room afterwards, and we knew then that another win in the second match of Folkestone Week, which began the very next day, would make the title all but ours.

Leicestershire were the visitors and we put in the sort of performance which showed the rest of the competition that we did not intend to be denied. John Shepherd took five wickets and Bob Woolmer three as they were bowled out on a blameless pitch for 152, and then we set about building a match-winning total with great elan. Mike and I kicked it off with a stand of 98, Graham Johnson made 108, Asif 63 in a wonderfully entertaining hour at the crease, and Shepherd and Ealham also hit out attractively. With Woolmer coming out to bat at number nine - what riches! - we eventually declared at 421-7 and with an invaluable eight batting points in the bag. Now the scene was set for Derek Underwood, and as ever he did not disappoint. When Leicestershire were all out for 229, and we had won by an innings and 40 runs, Derek had claimed 6-58.

And so we travelled to the Oval, five days later on September 9, knowing that we needed just six points for the championship. Lancashire, our nearest rivals, were 17 points behind and the first thing we noticed on arrival at Kennington was the green colour of the pitch! Even so, it would be fair to say that our captain needed some reassurance from the rest of the team before deciding to put Surrey in, although the fall of John Edrich to the first ball of the match merely underlined that it was the only decision he could really have made. Surrey were 151-9 at the close of that rain-shortened opening day, Woolmer taking 5-40 and Shepherd 3-70, but Micky Stewart declared overnight to deny us a fifth bowling point. That meant two batting points were required to clinch the title, and Asif and myself were more than happy to play supporting roles as Colin Cowdrey sealed our great triumph with one of his elegant and seemingly effortless centuries. I was out for 51, to make us 88-3, but Colin and Asif were still together in their lovely fourth wicket stand of 121 when the crucial second batting point was gained. It did not matter then that the match fizzled out as a draw. Cowdrey threw Kentish hops from the pavilion balcony to our supporters below, and we were champions!

Colin, by the way, had also made sure that 15 of the 18 players who had contributed to the championship success were at the Oval on the morning after the title was clinched for a special team photograph. It is a picture I treasure, especially because no fewer than 12 of those players were Kent-produced. The exceptions, of course, were Asif, Shepherd and Norman Graham, but by then they were all so much a part of the Kent scenery that they felt like homegrown players too!

It had been a tremendous thrill to win the 1967 Gillette Cup, but this was something again. You only have to talk to any professional cricketer to realise what winning the championship itself means. This was also Kent's first championship for 57 years, remember, and it was a pinnacle in all our careers.

Most excited of all, however, in that deliriously-happy Kent dressing room at the Oval on September 10, 1970, was Colin Cowdrey. All of us players knew how much Colin had wanted to experience this moment, and we knew how much work he had put into the development of the team since his appointment as captain in 1957. He, Les Ames and Colin Page were the three architects of that great victory, and I know our skipper was certainly a man who would also have been aware of the significance of the success in terms of Kent cricket history. He had fulfilled his ambition, but it was an ambition that went way beyond mere personal glory. Colin wanted so much to see Kent back at the top of the tree… and, after so much sweat and effort, we were there.

How much, too, we enjoyed flying the championship-winning pennant on top of pavilions at every one of our matches in 1971. In those days, the honour of flying that little flag made you very proud. Like all winners, we were feted afterwards, and it was nice to receive all the many letters from members, friends and supporters that come along. But there was little in the way of direct financial reward for winning in that era. Our real reward was to be able to fly the flag that told the world: look, we at Kent are the champions now!

Chapter 7
England

If Alan Knott had not run me out for 74 at the Gabba in Brisbane in November 1970, I could well have become the only Englishman since the War to score a hundred against Australia in my maiden Test innings. In fact, only four Englishmen have ever achieved that feat - W G Grace in 1880, R E Foster in 1903-04, George Gunn in 1907-08 and the Nawab of Pataudi senior on the Bodyline tour of 1932-33. Indeed, Graham Thorpe in 1993, and K S Ranjitsinhji, in 1896, are the only two others to have marked their England Test debuts with a century against Australia (they both did it in the second innings) so I really could have been in elite company if Knotty had not called me for that dodgy run!

Not that I am blaming Alan for it. For a start, I did not know at the time that it WAS actually my Test debut - I thought it was my sixth cap, because it was not until some time later that England's 1970 summer series against the Rest of the World was declared unofficial. And, even if I had known it was my debut, it still would not have mattered that much. At 31, I was just so happy to be having an England career at all. Most of all, too, I knew that my opportunity had only come along late in my cricketing life because of the tragic accident in 1969 that had befallen that gentle giant, Colin Milburn.

'Ollie' Milburn, as the roly-poly but brilliant Geordie batsman from Northamptonshire was universally known, played just nine Tests. English cricket was thus robbed of one of the brightest stars of that generation when Milburn lost his left eye in a car crash soon after beginning the 1969 season with an innings of 158 for Northants which contained five sixes. The previous winter, playing for Western Australia against Queensland, he had hit 243 before tea on the opening day.

But it was in the wake of Milburn's car accident that my name began to get circulated in newspaper stories speculating about future England teams. Indeed, 1969 was my best-ever season for Kent, and during the second half of the summer I began to believe that the press stories had some substance.

I was more than disappointed, therefore, when I was not selected for any of the three Tests England played against New Zealand in July and August, having beaten West Indies 2-0 in the first three-Test series of that summer. Mike Denness' call-up for the final Test against the Kiwis, at the Oval, was another fillip for Kent cricket, of course, and I was delighted that Mike marked his England debut by scoring 55 not out in the second innings as New Zealand were beaten by eight wickets and that series was also secured 2-0. But, in my private moments, I also knew that Mike's selection underlined just how close I myself had come to a precious first Test match cap.

Mike's age - he is 21 months younger than me - left me wondering, too, if the fact that I was by then 30 had mitigated against me in the selectors' minds. Playing for England had suddenly become a realistic dream in 1969, not merely a secret hope, but was it a brutal truth that I was just a year or two too old to be starting an international career?

In that 1969 summer I experienced exactly what current Kent captain David Fulton endured in 2001 - his own most prolific season in county cricket. David was

Above: Meeting the Queen at Lord's during England's Test match against India in 1971

Left: John Courage, the brewers, gave me this trophy in recognition of the hundred I made with a broken finger against Australia in the Melbourne Test of 1970-71

being constantly talked up by the newspapers as a candidate for that season's series against the Australians, but never actually got the call. That is what happened to me during most of 1969, and I remember ringing David to give him my support at one stage in that 2001 summer. I advised him to ignore the paper talk and keep his head down, because back in 1969 I definitely reacted in the wrong way to being pushed forward in the press. Then, I began to convince myself that I deserved England selection, where in fact these things have absolutely nothing to do with the media. It is the chairman of selectors, and his committee, who make these decisions… no-one else. I wanted David Fulton to be aware of my experience, and not to make the same mistake as I did and get too wrapped up in all the speculation surrounding you. At that stage in 2001, of course, I was hoping that David too would go on to experience what I did: which was, eventually, to get the international call-up that hard work and success alone can bring.

There was no England winter tour in 1969-70, either, and so I was frustrated and disappointed when I reached the end of a 1969 summer in which I had personally been so successful but which had not brought the rewards I had been hoping for on both a Kent and England level. But then, as the winter months began, I began to realise that at least I WAS being talked about, and that if I worked just a little bit harder, my chance might yet come. Colin Milburn's injury had still left a very large hole in the England 'squad' set-up, and an opportunity would still exist the following summer if I continued to play well.

After eight successive seasons in the Kent first team, I had in fact reached a new level as a county cricketer. I was now a county player with realistic England ambitions rather than being what I had been for so long… that is, a cricketer driven solely by the need to keep hold of a professional career in the game. In the mid-1960's, I had often told myself that my aim was to be good enough to enjoy a 10-year run in county cricket. If I could just play for Kent for 10 years… well, what a joy that would be! Suddenly, however, in 1969, my horizons widened. The realisation, also sudden, that I was now an established member of a still-improving Kent team did wonders for my self-confidence. My experience, by then, gave me an extra layer of self-belief, if you like, and perhaps that was why I had blossomed out as a batsman.

The other reason, undoubtedly, was the introduction in 1969 of the Sunday League. This was an immediate success around the counties, attracting big crowds far and wide, and as an opening batsman I found myself having to play in a manner in 40-over cricket that was wholly different from the method I had grown up with. Yes, I had by then played six years of Gillette Cup cricket - including our 1967 trophy-winning season - but the Sunday League introduced a regular diet of helter-skelter limited-overs cricket into the domestic game. The 40-over league arrived at just the right time for me, as I can appreciate now. I was experienced enough by 1969 to have the confidence to adapt, and I was sufficiently insured by my seniority against the fear of failure to be able to approach its new challenge in a totally positive manner.

Colin Cowdrey was also at this time a major source of encouragement to me. Colin was always very good at picking the right time to have a little word with his players, and also at saying the right things by way of encouragement. It is not after you have made a hundred, for example, that you need people telling you how good you are. But, if you have been on the receiving end of a few good deliveries, and have gone a couple of weeks without a run, it is fantastic when someone you respect takes the trouble of having a quiet word in your ear. All through my early career, Colin as captain would make sure he spoke at these important times to his players. With me, he kept on encouraging me to have belief in myself, and he kept on telling me I was a good batsman who could get even better.

Now, in 1969, here was one of the greatest batsmen England have ever had - and someone who had first played Test cricket 15 years earlier - telling me that I was good enough to play for England within the year, but that I still needed to be patient. Colin reminded me that I needed to concentrate solely on my game, and on gaining even more of the consistency that had begun to be more apparent in my cricket. He was right, of course, and it was his encouragement and kindness that did so much to prepare me mentally for the challenge of playing for England. By the time it really did happen, I had much more of the self-belief you require to do yourself justice at the highest level.

Several overseas trips also helped in my development as an opening batsman during the mid to late Sixties. In the winter of 1965-66, for instance, it was Colin who persuaded me that playing club cricket in South Africa would be good for me. But that first overseas experience of cricket, in the Johannesburg area, was followed by two much more important winter trips.

In January and February 1968, I had gone to Pakistan with a Commonwealth team led by Richie Benaud, and then in early 1970 I won selection for an International Cavaliers tour to Jamaica. Both trips gave me invaluable added experience, but the tour to the Caribbean enabled me to play some high standard winter cricket at a vital stage of my career. I got runs, too, with three hundreds in four innings, and felt very comfortable with my game and the way it was developing. Because of my lack of natural ability with the bat - compared to the Cowdreys of this world - I had concentrated on my role as being the Kent team's anchor man. I worked hard at occupying the crease, and providing the base around which other more talented players could express themselves. One-day cricket, however, and especially the Sunday League, forced me to throw off the popular image of me as being a blocker, and I enjoyed it immensely. In that first season of the Sunday League in 1969 I had not scored vast numbers of runs - it was 424 at an average of 30 - but I revelled in the greater freedom I felt out there in the middle.

The successes I enjoyed in Jamaica, batting against quality opposition, set me up nicely for the 1970 summer. It may even have provided that extra ounce of self-confidence which was about to propel me into the England team. But the way my life was about to change was dramatic. In the winters of 1968-69 and 1969-70 I had needed to work outside cricket, for the American company ARCO, in order to make ends meet. Their head office was in Ilford, and I was employed as a sales representative in east Kent, selling heating products and oil. That, of course, was itself quite a way above what I used to do as a teenager in the mid-1950's when I worked for several winters as a farm labourer at Gore Court cricketer Brian French's farm at Teynham! In the 1970-71 winter, however, I was about to be fully employed by going on an Ashes tour of Australia and being part of the England team which won back the famous urn for the first time in 14 years.

But I am getting ahead of myself! Geoff Boycott and John Edrich had opened the England innings throughout the summer of 1969, yet Ray Illingworth - who had taken over as captain when Colin Cowdrey ruptured his Achilles tendon during our Sunday League match at The Mote on May 25 - had begun 1970 still on the look-out for a third specialist opener to take to Australia that coming winter.

The 1970 summer was, for Illy, all about planning ahead for the Ashes. The scheduled visit by South Africa had been called off, for political reasons, and England were instead facing a five-match series against a Rest of the World XI. At the time, these matches were treated as full-on Tests, but in Illingworth's eyes they were also about getting the preparation right for Australia. The likes of Tom Graveney, Ted Dexter and Ken Barrington had all retired from Test cricket in 1968 or 1969, and Milburn's injury had cruelly forced out one of the natural successors to a top order batting place from the selectors' plans. In addition to this, both Boycott and Cowdrey requested some time out of international cricket in early 1970 - Geoffrey because of what he felt was a worrying lack of form and Colin because he was still getting back to full fitness following his Achilles problems of the previous season.

So it was that the England side for the opening Test against the Rest of the World offered some rare opportunity, and my form in the early weeks of the season was just about good enough to put me, once again, in the frame. On Friday June 12 the team for the first Test was due to be announced, but the radio in Mike Denness' car (there were no sponsored cars in those days!) was not working and the two of us remained blissfully unaware of the Test selection news as we made our way home from a Kent championship match against Hampshire at Portsmouth. Both of us, of course, were harbouring hopes of a call-up, but I don't recall us talking about it much on our way home. Mike had made his England debut in the final match of the 1969 season, but there was no guarantee that either of us would be chosen. In that situation, and especially when the two of you might just be competing for one place, you tend to chat about everything else other than Test selection!

Anyway, when Mike dropped me off at my house in Tunstall, near Sittingbourne, my wife did not say anything to me until we had waved Mike on his way. She had heard my name read out when the England team was announced on the radio earlier that evening, but she could not remember hearing Mike's name. So she did not tell me the news until Mike had driven off, in case he had asked about himself and she would have been unable to tell him. There was then no such thing as Ceefax, of course, and no-one from the England selection committee or from Lord's ever rang to tell you anything in advance! You just had to rely on the media announcements, like everyone else! We then waited to listen to the 10pm news bulletin, both to confirm my own selection and to hear that Mike too had been included. I rang him immediately, as by now he would have reached home himself, to offer my congratulations and receive his.

The first Test against the Rest of the World began on June 17, and was played at Lord's. I still regard it as my Test debut, in fact, as in my eyes I played 26 Tests for England and not 21... despite what the record books now show. The Rest of the World team was incredibly strong, and it is to that England side's credit that we could easily have forced a drawn series. I opened in the first Test with Alan Jones, of Glamorgan, who had been called up as a replacement because of a hand injury to John Edrich, and it was to be poor Alan's only England appearance. Imagine how sorry we all felt for him, one of the best players of his generation, when the matches were subsequently declared unofficial and even his solitary Test cap was taken away from him.

The first bowlers I had to face as an international batsman were Garth McKenzie, Mike Procter and Garry Sobers. McKenzie, the Australian, was as strong as an ox and really hit the pitch hard. Procter, then a young fast bowler who had been allowed just seven Test appearances by his country's apartheid regime, was very rapid and dangerous, while Sobers was at his very peak as the greatest all-round cricketer the world has seen. The ball swung around alarmingly, and we lost a couple of early wickets, but I hung on for about 50 minutes for one before I got an inswinger from Sobers and whipped it off my pads. Barry Richards, fielding at short leg, swung himself around in reflex self-defence and the ball hit him squarely in the small of his back. It bounced up into the air, and Barry swivelled around again and caught the rebound! My debut innings for England was over.

In the second innings, however, I made 67 and added 101 for the third wicket with Basil D'Oliveira. Wisden records that "Luckhurst used his feet well to the spinners", and I felt happy enough with the way I had played despite the fact that the Rest of the World won the match. Looking back, it was such an experience to be playing my first Test cricket against the likes of Sobers, Richards, Graeme Pollock, Eddie Barlow, Clive Lloyd and Lance Gibbs. What a line-up they had, with Procter down to bat most times at number nine! In terms of bowling quality, which is what I was most concerned about of course, I think it must rank as the best seam attack to take on England until the Australians put Lillee, Thomson and Max Walker into the field against us in 1974-75.

The second Test, at Trent Bridge, went even better for me - and much better for the team. In an excellent, close-fought contest, we levelled the series at 1-1 and I added an unbeaten 113 to my first innings 37. In the end, we won by eight wickets, but it was always closer than that, as the Rest of the World's totals of 276 and 286 and our first innings of 279 tell you. Alec Bedser, then chairman of selectors, came into our dressing room just before the start of our second innings and told me: "I don't care how long we take to get these runs - I just want to win it!" And this from a man who, three years earlier, had dropped Geoff Boycott from Test cricket for scoring too slowly when he made 246 not out against India in a match England also won!

Anyway, I batted for a shade under seven hours and we eventually got home with four overs to spare. It was a joyful day for me, of course, and I think it was appropriate that Colin Cowdrey marked his return to England colours with an innings of 64 as we put on 120 for the second wicket. Colin had been so instrumental in the way I had improved as a batsman, and now here we were putting on a match-winning stand together for our country! "When England batted a second time, Luckhurst's unbreachable defence and Cowdrey's return to form soon removed most doubts about the eventual outcome", says Wisden.

The Rest of the World won the third Test at Edgbaston by five wickets, but their two-wicket victory in the next Test at Headingley was very hard for us to take. Boycott had returned for this match, having told Illy he was feeling better about his game, and in a forerunner of the coming winter John Edrich dropped down to number three to accommodate Geoff and I at the top of the order. We put on 37 and 104 together in that match, and it was the start of a very productive and enjoyable opening partnership. Not that running with Geoff was all that easy! I was used to Mike Denness, with whom I had a brilliant understanding, so it was quite unnerving when - with our total still 0 - Geoff began our alliance by pushing a ball from Procter square on the offside and shouting "Yes!". I started to run, but then he saw the predatory figure of Clive Lloyd making giant strides towards the ball. "No!" he cried, but then shouted "There is a run, yes!", without breaking stride. As we passed in mid-pitch, with me with my head down in a desperate attempt to get to the other end, he hissed: "Run, you silly little man!" It wasn't particularly funny at the time, but luckily Lloyd uncharacteristically fumbled and I often have a chuckle to myself about what Geoff said when I now see or hear him commentating. Later, I remember us sitting down quietly in the corner of the dressing room and discussing our approach to running between the wickets. We had a good chat about it, and after that we never had another problem. I enjoyed batting with Geoff immensely, and in 16 Test innings as an opening pair we averaged 51.5 together, which isn't too bad by

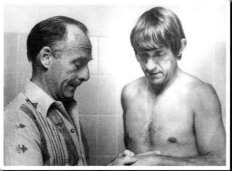

Bernard Thomas, the England physiotherapist, examines the damage done during my Melbourne century in 1970-71

This photograph captures the moment that I was run out at Brisbane in my first official Test

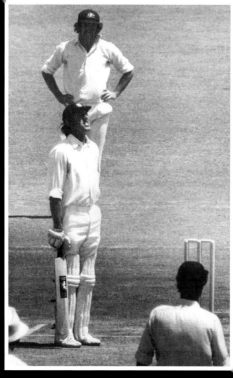

"Are we going to get on with this effing game, or not?" That was the message that I am receiving here from Ian Chappell, the Australian captain, at Perth in 1974-75

The Test debut that never was. At the time of this photograph, taken before England's first match against the Rest of the World at Lord's in June 1970, I thought I was about to win my first Test cap. From left to right (back row): Alan Jones, myself, Derek Underwood, Alan Ward, Ken Shuttleworth, Mike Denness, (front row) Basil D'Oliveira, John Snow, Ray Illingworth (captain), Phil Sharpe, Alan Knott any standards.

We would have won the Leeds game, meanwhile, if a clear bat-pad catch offered by Barry Richards had been given while he and Procter were taking the Rest of the World team from 183-8 in their second innings to a winning 226-8. Richards was batting low down the order because of injury, but he was reprieved off the slow left-arm spin of Don Wilson and he and Procter saw them home. It could, and perhaps should, have been 2-2 that evening but at 3-1 down - and with just one match left - we had instead lost the series. Eddie Barlow took four wickets in five balls in that game, by the way, including a hat-trick. And just look at the Rest of the World team which faced us at Headingley: Richards, Barlow, Kanhai, Mushtaq Mohammad, G Pollock, Lloyd, Sobers, Procter, Intikhab Alam, Deryck Murray, Gibbs. How did we ever come so close to winning?

I got 92 at Headingley, too, before I tried to clip away a ball from Barlow which pitched just in the bowlers' rough outside the line of my leg stump and stopped a bit on me. The result was a catch to mid-wicket, which was a little disappointing, but after my first four England appearances I had 408 runs under my belt. After the fifth and final Test at the Oval, though, I still had 408!

The Rest of the World won there, too, to take the series 4-1, and a total of 53,000 people still turned up to watch over the five days even though there was nothing really riding on the result. Of chief concern to me at the time, however, was the fact that I bagged a pair - clean bowled by Mike Procter in both innings, third ball and first ball. I remember vividly walking off the field after the second nought thinking to myself that I had blown my chances of touring Australia, and after such a good series and such a lot of hard work as well. In fact, on the morning before my second duck, I travelled to the ground from the team hotel in the same car as Ray Illingworth. Illy remarked that I would be "on a pair" when our second innings began and asked me, in that joshing way that sportsmen have, when I had last suffered a pair in first-class cricket. "Skipper," I replied, "I have never got a pair in a first-class match", which was then true, "and, what is more, I don't intend to get one today either!" Talk about famous last words.

Later that day, when I had unstrapped my pads and gone for a quiet sit to watch the game going on without me, I felt a hand on my shoulder. It was Andy Sandham, the old Surrey and England opening batsman, who was then a fit and jaunty 80. "Feeling sorry for yourself, son?" said the old cricketer in commiseration, and when I nodded and smiled thinly he added: "But if you think you were unlucky then what about what happened to me the last time I was on a pair on this ground?" Sandham then went on to tell me the story of how he had gone out to bat on a pair and found that a third floor flat window, outside the ground, was open at such an angle that the sun was shining off it straight into his eyes! As the bowler was running in, he had to pull away as the reflection was blinding. "I apologised both to the umpire and the bowler, who was almost into his delivery stride at the time," said Sandham, "and the umpire said he was going to go and sort it out. He ran from the field, found a policeman who was patrolling around the ground and instructed the policeman to get on to his bicycle and go to the block of flats responsible. We all waited until the policeman had made it up to the third floor and had shut the window. Only then did play restart… and I still got out for a pair!"

After that Test I endured an excruciating week or so waiting to see who the selectors would choose for the Ashes tour to Australia. There were quite a number of certainties of course: Boycott, for instance, had scored 157 at the Oval and Peter Lever had come up on the rails for one of the fast bowling places by taking 7-83 in that last match against the Rest of the World. Colin Cowdrey would be there as vice-captain to Illingworth, and there was no way that the likes of Knott, Underwood, Edrich, Snow and D'Oliveira would be missing from the squad. When the tour party names were announced, it was a huge moment in my career to see mine amongst them. The only sadness, from both a personal and a Kent point of view, was that Mike Denness did not make the list. He was pipped by John Hampshire of Yorkshire for the final batting place.

We were soon on our way to Australia, and for me this was the ultimate in cricket... especially if we could win back those Ashes! But more excitement was to follow on our arrival Down Under, because it quickly became apparent that Illy wanted Boycott and myself to open, with Edrich at three. I had assumed I was going as the reserve opener, because the other two were so much more experienced and battle-hardened than me at that level, but soon John was being asked by Ray if he would be happy doing the job at first wicket down. My Test place was assured from the moment, in the very first game of the tour, we beat a South Australian Country XI by 10 wickets in a one-day fixture and Geoff Boycott and I put on 148. I had also outscored Geoff by 18 runs, with an unbeaten 82 to his 64 not out, but, after we had both marched off unbeaten and the lads had started ribbing him about it, he stood up and said: "Well, I'm not surprised Brian scored a few more because, actually, he faced 12 more balls than me!" And do you know what, I secretly checked with our scorer later how many deliveries each of us had indeed faced, and Geoffrey - unbelievably - had been exactly right!

After doing well in the first Test, I then really cemented my position at the top of the order by scoring a hundred against Western Australia in the run-up to the second Test. Tony Lock, the old England left-arm spinner, was playing for them and when I got to 96 I said to him: "Locky, one more four and I'm all yours." He smiled, delivered a full toss which I whacked for four and then, two balls later, smiled again when I got myself out! A very young and raw Dennis Lillee opened the WA bowling against us in that match - something I was not aware of until much later. In view of how my Test career ended, of course, it is now nice to be able to say that I managed to score at least one hundred off Lillee!

Geoff Boycott and I put on 92 in the first innings of the opening Ashes Test, at Brisbane, and then Alan Knott came in to join me as nightwatchman at the end of the second day's play. The following day, we took our second wicket stand to 44 before the run out incident that was to deny me the chance of that historic debut hundred. But even if I'd known that this was actually going to go in the record books as my Test debut, and not my sixth cap as I thought at the time, I still would have been run out! I had, in truth, got a bit bogged down and, on 74, pushed a ball from leg-spinner Terry Jenner around the corner. The next thing I knew was that Knotty was halfway down the pitch yelling "Yes" and, as it was his call, I set off. But the ball had gone straight to the fielder and, because of my hesitation, I was comfortably out by two or three yards when the ball was flung to the bowler's end.

I greatly enjoyed that first Test, however, and I ended up with 20 not out in the second innings as the match meandered to a draw despite us bowling them out for 214 on the final day. Ken Shuttleworth, the Lancashire fast bowler, got a five-wicket haul on his Test debut and John Snow took six wickets in the Australian first innings to lay down his marker for what was going to be the greatest series of his distinguished career. Snow was genuinely quick on that trip, and I was tickled during that Brisbane Test when Lou Rowan, then Australia's leading umpire, warned him for bowling what he termed too many 'bouncers'. Snowy protested that they were merely short balls, not bouncers, and indeed the fact was that they were so wickedly accurate that the Aussie batsmen were being drawn into trying to fend off most of them. Anyway, there was an animated debate about it for a while, before Snow marched back to his mark. There then followed a very fast short-pitched ball which took off and flew high into Knotty's gloves as the batsman ducked under it. With a big grin on his face, Snow turned around to Rowan at the end of his follow-through and said: "THAT'S a bouncer, Lou!"

I'm not going to chronicle all my England Test appearances in fine detail, but the second Test of that 1970-71 tour provided me with a really special moment - the first of my four Test centuries. As I've said before, of course, I thought at the time that it was my second - following the Trent Bridge hundred against the Rest of the World - but that certainly didn't make it any less special when I reached those three figures in Perth! Boycott and I put on 171 for the first wicket, and again I'd like to point out that I outscored Geoffrey before he was out for 70! I went on to 131, and I treasure the film I have at home of the Australian players, led by Ian Chappell and Rod Marsh, clapping me on my hundred. As this was the first Test match ever played at Perth, by the way, my name is now at the top of the honours board that has recently been put up in the visiting dressing-room at the WACA. On that board, similar to one that is at Lord's, is a list of all the overseas players who have either made a century or taken five wickets or more in a Perth Test. It was a thrill for me to see it on my last visit to the ground two years ago.

We won the fourth Test at Sydney, after the scheduled third Test at Melbourne had been abandoned without a ball being bowled due to torrential rain, and once again Boycott and I launched our first innings solidly with a stand of 116. Geoff made 77 and 142 not out in this match, and Snow finished off Australia with 7-40 in their second innings. Throughout the series those two were our trump cards, although I am proud of my other contributions and in particular my 109 in the fifth Test at Melbourne, during which I broke the little finger of my left hand. But it was important that I stayed out there, after we had struggled to 88-3 in reply to Australia's 493-9 declared, and Basil D'Oliveira also scored a hundred as the two of us put on 140 for the fourth wicket. It was such a thrill to do well in front of a massive crowd of 70,000 people, then a world record gate in terms of money for the third day of a Test match.

Eventually that game was drawn, as was the next Test which I missed because of my fractured finger. But how glad I am that I had recovered in time to play in the rescheduled third Test (or seventh Test as it became known) at the Sydney Cricket Ground. I got a duck in the first innings, after coming back in for the injured Boycott, but both my new opening partner Edrich and I made second innings fifties in a vital partnership of 94 which wiped off an awkward 80-run deficit. After finally managing to set the Australians 223 to square the series and save the Ashes, we bowled them out for 160 despite Snow breaking a finger in a collision with the boundary fence soon after taking the first wicket of the innings. Derek Underwood and Ray Illingworth took five wickets between them, and D'Oliveira chipped in with a couple too as we worked our way steadily through the Aussie batting. It was obviously an extremely tense match, especially after Illy led us off in protest late on the second day after Snow had hit Terry Jenner on the head with a bouncer and the crowd began to throw cans of beer on to the outfield. But I had never experienced anything as tense as the final morning of the match. Australia got to 131-5 overnight, with Keith Stackpole hitting 67, but when Knotty beautifully stumped Greg Chappell for 30 off Illingworth, to one that turned through the gate, and

Underwood bowled Marsh, it was always going to be our game, and our Ashes.

On the night before the final morning, though, I simply could not get to sleep - despite having taken two sleeping tablets. When we went out on to the field, I then found myself almost willing the ball not to come to me - such was the tension and the fear of doing something stupid like dropping a vital catch. And, don't forget, I loved fielding and had the reputation of being one of the safest catchers around! In the end, I was at gully when Jenner was caught by Keith Fletcher at silly point off Underwood. We had won the series 2-0, and we chaired Ray Illingworth from the field. What a moment that was - and how quickly did the beers in our dressing room fridge disappear afterwards! I swapped caps with Rod Marsh, who I later realised made his Test debut at the same time as me, and February 17, 1971, will remain as one of the proudest days of my life.

The next day saw us fly on to New Zealand, where we were to play two Tests in a three-week stay, and one of the funniest memories I have of that incredible four and a half month adventure involved our final night in Australia. I had spent the late afternoon back in the hotel trying to sleep off the celebratory lunchtime beers we had sunk at the ground, but Basil D'Oliveira was one of the players who had decided to keep on drinking. Basil had a good friend in Sydney, a top surgeon, and he had invited both of us along to his house that evening for a farewell dinner - also attended by the rest of his family, his two children and his parents. You can imagine how happy Dolly was by the time we were all sitting around the dinner table, and what I most remember most about a fairly hazy evening is that Basil kept saying "Lucky - we stuffed the bastards!" over and over again.

It was, of course, a magnificent achievement to go to Australia and win back the Ashes - as more recent history has proved only too well - and do you know that no lbw appeal was upheld against an Australian batsman in that entire Test series? A coincidence, I'm sure, but it just underlines how hard we had to fight for our success... and how sweet it was to emerge as only the fourth England team to have regained the Ashes on Australian soil.

Like the England rugby team at last year's World Cup in Australia, we had also taken a lot of stick for being a 'Dad's Army' outfit, but we had done the business when it mattered most, and we had stood up well to the physical and mental strains of being away from home on such a long tour. Remarkably, our only first-class victories on the whole Australian leg of the tour were the two Test wins... but who cares? Again, as the rugby boys will tell you, it is only the results in the really big games that people remember anyway.

I was 32 by the time I returned from New Zealand, but overjoyed that I was now a fully-fledged England cricketer under a captain in Illingworth who was undoubtedly the best I have played for. Despite scoring two more Test hundreds, against Pakistan and India in the following 1971 summer, and playing against the Aussies again in the 1972 and 1974-75 Ashes series, the 1970-71 tour was the clear pinnacle of my career. In simple terms, indeed, what else could beat it? Back in England after the tour, all of us were invited to go to Fortnum and Masons in London to bottle our own commemorative half-case of Taylor's vintage port. We have drunk five of them, but I still can't bring myself to open the last one! It just sits there at home... itself a proud reminder of the time we travelled all the way to Australia and won back the Ashes for England.

Chapter 8

Glory Years

When Denis Compton swept the boundary which clinched the Ashes for England at the Oval in 1953, it was the stuff of dreams for the 14-year old boy watching entranced from beyond the ropes. Yet even as I sat cheering excitedly as Australia were beaten for the first time for 20 years, it would still have required a wild imagination for me to picture myself as the batsman out there hitting the Ashes-winning runs. On July 29, 1972, however, at 5.04pm, that man was indeed me.

The moment that schoolboy dreams are made of came true for the then 33-year old England opener late on the third day of the fourth Test of that summer's Ashes series. We went into the rubber as holders of the Ashes, of course, following the triumphs of the 1970-71 tour, and that Headingley Test began with us level with the Aussies at 1-1. But, on a controversial pitch, Derek Underwood took 4-37 and 6-45 as Australia were bowled out for 146 and 136, and soon John Edrich and I were walking out to open our second innings with only 20 runs needed for the victory that would ensure the Ashes stayed in England. John fell lbw to Dennis Lillee for four, but from the last ball of the tenth over I swept an off-break from Ashley Mallett to the fine leg boundary - probably with not quite the style of Compton! - for the runs that retained the Ashes.

Little did I know, though, as I left the field to join the celebrations of another job well done by Ray Illingworth and his team, that my own England career was never going to be the same again.

Illingworth had indicated that he wanted to take the subsequent winter off, when a tour of India and Pakistan was scheduled, and Tony Lewis was appointed as a caretaker captain. As a clear pointer to the thinking of the new regime for the winter ahead, Barry Wood of Lancashire was brought in to open, in my place, and got 90 in the second innings of the fifth and final Test - even though England were beaten to leave the series drawn at 2-2. Neither Edrich or Geoff Boycott was available for that winter's tour, but if I thought that made me a certainty for one of the opening positions then I was sadly mistaken.

It was not as if I had failed during the first four Tests of the 1972 Ashes series, however. I may not have scored heavily, but my second innings 96 in the third Test at Trent Bridge was England's highest individual score of the summer. Perhaps things would have been different if I had managed to get the extra four runs I needed for a fifth Test century, although I can't believe that such a mere cosmetic factor would have changed much. As it was, I tried to work away a leg-break from Ian Chappell, an occasional bowler operating from around the wicket into the rough outside leg stump, and thick-edged to gully. I still think now about the low full toss Chappell bowled to me earlier in that same over, which I caught right on the bottom of the bat as I tried to drive it wide of mid-on for four! I wonder if my winter of 1972-73 would have been spent in the sub-continent if that ball had flown from the middle of my bat and not been stubbed into the ground…

As it was, I nevertheless could still not work out why they would want to take batsmen like Barry Wood to India and Pakistan, and not me. That's not being unkind to Barry, who was a fine and gutsy cricketer but who had a big reputation as a player of pace and not the spin bowling that was going to be the major danger on sub-continental pitches. I was very happy against the spinners, and had made Test centuries against both India and Pakistan in the previous summer of 1971.

Suffice to say here, I was bitterly disappointed not to make the 1972-73 tour, and I regard the eight Tests that England played that winter as a huge missed opportunity for me. I was also a little upset at not being selected for the following winter's tour to the West Indies, but at least before that 1973-74 trip I was given two summer Tests against the same opposition and didn't get the runs I needed to make sure of a place. Looking back, though, it was a nonsense that I subsequently found myself taking on Lillee and Thomson in 1974-75 in Australia, but played no overseas Tests at all between early 1971 and late 1974.

On the 1972-73 tour, by the way, England ended up dropping Barry Wood after three Tests of the initial series against India. He scored only 101 runs from six innings, with a top score of 45, and was dismissed four times by Bishen Bedi and once by Chandrasekhar! In the fourth Test the England opening pair were Graham Roope and Mike Denness, while in the fifth Test Roope and Lewis opened in the first innings and the barely-believable partnership of Roope and off-spinner Jack Birkenshaw in the second! Wood was eventually only recalled for the third and final Test against Pakistan, after being sidelined for almost two months, and scored just three and five. I rest my case!

If Illingworth had been captain that winter I think I would have gone, but for whatever reason perhaps Tony Lewis didn't fancy me in the mix of players he wanted to take with him - and so I missed out. With Illingworth resuming the captaincy for the summer of 1973, however, I won a recall for the last two Tests of the three-match West Indies series. England had thrashed New Zealand 2-0 earlier in the summer, but Illy suddenly came under pressure when the first Test against the West Indians was lost by 158 runs. I was brought back to bat at number three, behind the now established opening partnership of Boycott and Dennis Amiss, and scores of 12 and 42 were not too bad as we drew the second Test, at Edgbaston.

But then, at Lord's, in the final Test, it all went wrong. We were pulverised by an innings and 226 runs, after Rohan Kanhai, Garry Sobers and Bernard Julien all scored hundreds in a West Indies total of 652-8 declared, and Illingworth resigned. On a personal level, I made only one and 12, and I knew when my second innings ended early on the fourth morning that I would not be on the plane to the Caribbean that winter.

The main memory I have of my last home Test, though, is an incident involving Boycott just before the end of play on the third day. We had by then been forced to follow on, and Alan Knott was sent in ahead of me as a nightwatchman when Amiss fell early to Keith Boyce. But Knotty also got out to Boyce, and I went in at 38-2 with just a couple of overs left. It was murky light, too, and in a subsequent little mid-pitch conference I asked Geoffrey if he wouldn't mind trying to see out the final over from Boyce as I was struggling to adjust to the light, having just come in and faced only two balls. He muttered something, but then got down to the task of seeing out the last over with what looked from my end to be comparative ease. From the final ball of the day, however, Boyce tempted Geoff into a rash hook - and, shockingly for all concerned, our number one batsman was caught at long leg. As he walked off past me, his face like thunder, Geoff said to me: "Happy now, are you?" and he was still chuntering away in the dressing room afterwards until Illy told him to be quiet!

The follow-up to this story is equally amusing, because Geoffrey didn't utter a single word in my direction from then until the following August, 1974, when I was captaining Kent in a Sunday League game against his Yorkshire side at Headingley. England's winter tour selection had just been made, and Boycott's name was in the tour squad. But as we walked out to toss up before the game, Geoff and I exchanged a few pleasantries before he suddenly said to me, in a sarcastic but knowing tone: "Well, Brian, good luck today - and send me a postcard from Sydney, won't you!"

I thought he was joking, at first, but then I realised that it was his way of telling me he wouldn't be going to Australia, especially of course because Mike Denness was still England captain and he wasn't, and that he had heard a whisper that I would get the nod as his 'deputy'. I also like to think, because we do have a lot of respect for each other, that it was his way of endorsing my selection in his place. As it was, I phoned Mike Denness the next morning to advise him to check with Lord's about whether Geoffrey had returned his signed tour contract. That was when it was discovered, officially, that Geoff had decided not to go and, about a week later, when I was already on an end-of-season holiday in Spain, it was announced that I had been selected as Boycott's replacement. I only heard about my call-up, though, on Radio Luxembourg as the letter that Lord's had sent out to me had ended up at another place in Spain called Callela - and not the Callela where myself, my wife and the boys were staying!

'Boycs' never did get that postcard from Sydney, by the way, because when I got out there and had to face Lillee and Thomson in their prime I soon began to say to myself: "Why aren't you here, Geoffrey, because this should be your job - not mine!"

The 1974-75 tour was a trip too far for me and, at 36 by the time it ended, I don't think in all seriousness I should have been there. Sure, replacing Boycott with myself was a like-for-like selection in the eyes of the management, but I had not really been in the front of the England selectors' minds since the summer of 1972. The England team needed Boycott, to be honest, but if not it needed a pair of eyes - and reflexes - that were younger than mine.

Not that I didn't give it my best. And not, in a strange way, that I don't appreciate now having had the chance to witness the Lillee and Thomson phenomenon at close quarters. It was not pleasant, I can tell you, but it gave me an insight into how Test cricket was changing. To look back at us walking out there in those pre-helmet days to face two of the fastest and most dangerous bowlers the world has seen - on lightning-quick and bouncy surfaces - still provides almost a ghoulish fascination. And, given everything, my two last Test scores of 27 and 23, made in the second Test at Perth, one of the quickest and bounciest pitches in the world, represent not the worst way to bow out of international cricket.

I did not enjoy that tour, though, especially after I was left out of the Test side and it became blindingly obvious to me that I would not get a Test recall when we went on to New Zealand at the end of the Australia series. David Lloyd, Colin Cowdrey and Bob Willis had all returned home instead of going on to New Zealand and Barry Wood - yes, him again! - was flown out to join the squad for the New Zealand leg. Soon after our arrival in New Zealand, and after I had played in the warm-up match against Wellington, Wood was chosen ahead of me for the opening Test despite having been there just three days following his 63-hour journey from a cricket trip in the West Indies. I therefore asked the England management to allow me to go home too. They refused and, in the first Test

Sharing a drink with Alec Bedser, the England manager, on the 1974-75 tour to Australia

A pull for four off Yorkshire's Richard Hutton during the 1971 Gillette Cup second round at Canterbury

Receiving a new 1300 Volkswagen as a gift from Mr A Colborne-Baber, managing director of Colborne Garages at their Sturry, Canterbury branch in 1973. To quote what Mr Colborne-Baber said at the time: "Cricketers don't get 'Oscars', but the entertainment they give the public is more than equal to those who do and Brian deserves the highest possible award for his contribution.

Another celebration at Canterbury in the early 1970's

Being interviewed by Christopher Martin-Jenkins, after winning a man of the match award, is clearly a happy occasion

No prizes for guessing the identity of Father Christmas at the England team's festivities during the 1974-75 tour to Australia: Mike Denness is with the other member of a long-serving Kent opening partnership

Another great catch. In 1973, on a visit to the River Spey in Scotland, I was allowed to keep the 26-pounder that I am struggling to hold up in my left hand

Fishing with David Lloyd during the 1974-75 tour was a lot more pleasant than facing Lillee and Thomson

against the Kiwis, Wood got nought in an England total of 593-6 declared - and I got on to the field only as a substitute fielder.

That four-month tour felt like four years to me, whereas the 1970-71 Ashes trip of equal length had flown by. It was a shame that my England career had to end that way, and I felt I should have been given the opportunity - like the other top order batsmen in the squad - of being able to score runs against New Zealand after battling so hard in Australia. But I still remain honoured to have had the chance of representing England at all, and I am grateful for the experiences - both on and off the cricket field - that my two tours and 21 caps (26 if you include the Rest of the World series) gave me.

My last Test appearance at Perth also coincided with one of the most amazing international comebacks of all - that of Colin Cowdrey. It was a privilege to be there to see it, a great cricketer by then almost 42 years old walking out to take on Lillee and Thomson just four days after arriving from an English winter. Colin had been called up as an emergency replacement, following hand injuries to Dennis Amiss and John Edrich in the first Test, but had not played Test cricket since June 1971. His son Chris tells the story of how, then 17, he said to Colin at home: "Why on earth are you doing this, Dad?" Apparently, Colin just smiled and said: "Well, it might be fun!"

When I was out for 27, caught off Max Walker, Colin came out at number three (which in itself was surprising, to my mind) and we passed at the gate. There is film showing us chatting for about ten seconds or so before Colin continued on his way to great applause. It was soon after he reached the middle, of course, that he introduced himself to Jeff Thomson ("By the way, as we haven't met before, my name's Cowdrey. Pleased to meet you."). Thommo's reply was not quite so classy. Colin scored 22, too, helping David Lloyd to add a further 55 for the second innings, and in our second innings he displayed yet more skill and courage to make 41 as an opener due to the badly bruised hand which forced me to come in down at number seven.

Thomson had struck me a nasty blow on the back of my hand, and to make things worse he had hit me again on the same spot from the very next ball! It hurt a lot, I can tell you, and it took me a while before I could carry on. From the slip cordon came Ian Chappell's voice: "Are we going to get on with this f....... game, or not?" That was Chappell, I'm afraid, and that was how Test cricket - led largely by his team, it must be said - was then going. Spearheaded by Lillee, Thomson and Walker, the Australians were now the best team in the world, and they were about to claim back the Ashes as further proof of it. But they never behaved in the way that world champions, in my view, should behave. Sledging doesn't make you a tough-guy. It is only by taking on and being successful against the best that cricketers win my respect.

I played in eight Tests against Australia before being on the losing side, but in 1974-75 we came off very much second best, and the reason was Thomson and Lillee. To illustrate the difference they made you just have to look at what happened in the sixth and final Test at Melbourne. Thomson was out injured, and Lillee broke down after getting Dennis Amiss out for nought in a new ball spell of six overs. He didn't bowl again in the match, and from 18-2 we went on to total 529 and win the Test by an innings and four runs!

I remember one night that all five of us Kent boys went out to dinner together - myself, Colin, Mike Denness, Derek Underwood and Alan Knott - and we ended up having a fascinating discussion about the difficulty of competing against fast bowling of the ferocity and quality of Lillee and Thomson. This was Colin's sixth Ashes tour, don't forget, so we asked him to name a batting line-up drawn from all the England batsmen he had played with in Australia to take them on.

He considered all the great names, from Hutton and May to Graveney and Barrington and Boycott and Dexter, and said that he could not pick any top order capable of taking the attack back to Lillee and Thomson in those conditions. To a mere mortal like me, I suppose that was some compensation for the bruises I received!

The only thing that I can say, having seen a 42-year old Cowdrey bat against Lillee and Thomson, is that the very great players still have that split second more time in which to play the ball. It is a rare ability, indeed, although it doesn't of course make facing the fastest bowling easier or more pleasant. But whether they actually do have that extra time, or whether it is just an illusion created by their technique, does not much matter. That's what it looks like when they bat, and that is what sets them apart.

And, to illustrate just how much more dangerous Lillee and Thomson were in their own home conditions, you only have to fast forward slightly to our 1975 summer when Colin scored one of the most glorious hundreds of his entire career to take Kent to victory against the visiting Australians at Canterbury. On an English pitch, which was that much slower than Perth or Brisbane or Melbourne, he found he was hooking bouncers from Dennis Lillee way in front of square. In Australia those shots were going behind square leg - if you managed to get anything on the ball in the first place!

But if my last experiences with England were mainly unhappy ones - and I was truly unhappy when Alec Bedser, the tour manager, turned down my request to go home from New Zealand - then I enjoyed everything about my final years as a player at Kent.

Captaining the side in that historic 1975 win over the Australians was, personally, a very sweet moment. The Aussies had ordered their team bus to be ready by mid-afternoon on the final day, because they expected to be wrapping up a victory of their own by then. But Colin Cowdrey, well-supported by others, decided otherwise as he thrillingly led the chase to get 354 in five and a quarter hours. Bob Woolmer made 71 and young Charles Rowe also batted gallantly towards the end. But the stage belonged to Colin, who finished on 151 not out when we won by four wickets. It was a very satisfying experience for me to be able to walk down the pavilion steps and offer my hand and my commiserations to Ian Chappell ("Thanks, Ian, good game mate!") as he and his chastened Aussies trooped off behind the conquering Cowdrey at the end! The 1974-75 tour had left me in a bad state of mind for a while, but this was an experience to set the world right again.

＊　　＊　　＊　　＊

The pleasure of coming first is the greatest feeling of them all for a professional sportsman, but what also made Kent's success so exciting and fulfilling in the heady days of the 1970's was that we were so much a bunch of mates. Cricket, by definition, is an individual sport masquerading as a team sport: each ball is a contest between individuals and, as a batsman or bowler or fielder, no-one else can do it for you. Batting, in particular, is a lonely business at times and most successful cricketers need a selfish, self-absorbed streak in them in order to be able to deal with the stresses and strains of the job.

The Kent team, however, which grew up together through the initial Gillette

Cup triumph of 1967 and then the great 1970 championship win, was a team in the truest sense of the word. We were individual competitors, and we had individual ambitions, but we were friends too. We supported each other, and it was the strength of the group as much as the great ability of its constituent parts which made us a formidable opponent.

The 1971 Gillette Cup final is remembered above all else for the stunning catch at mid off by Lancashire captain Jack Bond which prevented Asif Iqbal from winning the match for Kent. What I most remember it for is letting myself become a self-induced victim of Peter Lever. Even now, I can't believe I allowed myself to be so stupid!

Lancashire and England fast bowler Peter, or 'Plank' to give him his universally-known nickname, was my roommate for more than 10 weeks of the previous winter's Ashes tour and we became firm friends. So much so that, as we sat together on the jubilant flight home from the tour, he warned me that he would bowl me a bouncer first ball if Kent came up against Lancashire in the coming season's Gillette Cup final at Lord's. And so, when fate decreed that we did indeed meet six months later on September 4, 1971, I remembered that conversation.

After walking out to open the Kent reply to Lancashire's 224-7 I found myself preparing to face the first ball of the innings… from Peter Lever. He hadn't said a word to me all match, and nor had I to him, but now there he was, rolling up his sleeves at the end of his mark and there I was, taking my guard and fighting to concentrate. As Peter ran in, I was thinking: "I remember, but does he?" Well, the first ball was a wide, good length ball, and as I had not exactly been expecting it I let it go through to the keeper. Peter's face didn't crack. Now, I thought, he's trying to wind me up. He's deliberately not showing anything, because he knows I think I know what's coming - and he's trying to out-think me! Anyway, the second delivery was also widish, and full, and so we went on through that opening over. By the time he bowled his fifth ball I didn't really know what to expect… but it was, in fact, a wide long hop and I decided to cut it. The result? Luckhurst c Engineer b Lever 0, and Kent's opening batsman out to a thin edge and walking back in front of a Lord's full house feeling very, very annoyed with himself. Afterwards, when we decided to drown our own sorrows by going along the Lord's pavilion corridor to congratulate Lancashire's players in their dressing room and then help them to drink their champagne, I sat myself down next to Peter and said: "Come on - what about that bouncer you promised me?" And Peter, turning to me with a genuine look of surprise, replied: "Oh yes, sorry Brian, I forgot!" I think my next words were something along the lines of "You plank, Lever!" but, in truth, perhaps they might have been just a little bit stronger than that!

Emotion-wise, though, that cup final was really all about Asif. Funnily enough, when we arrived at Lord's that morning, we were unusually tense. Sometimes, in a dressing room on the morning of a big match, there is something in the air which players can feel. Everyone quite naturally gets keyed up before an important game, but usually that is disguised quite well beneath the banter and the chatter. On that day, however, and despite our previous success at Lord's, something didn't seem quite right and Asif himself sensed it. He suddenly announced to everyone: "There is no need to worry, lads, because we are going to win today and I am going to win the man-of-the-match award!" That immediately lifted the tension, and I remember thinking how clever it was of Asif to do it in that way. Afterwards, though, when he was indeed awarded the man-of-the-match medal for his great but ultimately availing innings, we had to push him forward to collect it. He was so disappointed that we had lost that he just didn't want the award.

Norman Graham, on the other hand, was so distraught about losing the 1972 Gillette Cup semi-final, also to Lancashire and this time by seven runs rather than 24, that he refused to speak on our return home from Old Trafford. As I was the only other one in the car, it made for a very long journey. But that is how hard successful sports people sometimes take being on the losing side. It just comes out in different ways.

We also finished runners-up in the championship in 1972 but at least finished that season with some silverware after pipping Leicestershire by one point to take the Sunday League title. In fact, we won our last six matches - including against Leicestershire themselves by five runs at Gillingham on August 6 - and our final victory, against 1971 Sunday champions Worcestershire at Canterbury on September 10, attracted a 12,000 crowd. This time, Asif saw us home by five wickets with 21 not out after I had scored 67 and put on 108 for the third wicket with David Nicholls. By now Bernard Julien had joined us and our side was packed with all-rounders. Julien was extremely talented, but disappointing for us overall. He had the natural ability even to have been a worthy successor in the West Indies team to the great Garry Sobers.

In 1973 came both the Benson and Hedges Cup and Sunday League titles, and it was also my benefit year. I don't think I had a spare moment that summer, what with all that going on Kent-wise and making a short-lived England comeback when I was chosen for the last two Tests against the West Indies in August. I scored 79, Kent's top score, in our B&H final win against Worcestershire at Lord's, and also had a decent season with an average of 68 in the John Player League and 41 in the championship. I only give these figures because it is often the case for a county beneficiary to struggle on the field. There is just so much time involved in a benefit year that many players have found balancing the cricket and the functions difficult, so I am proud that I still managed to perform well out in the middle.

I must have enjoyed myself, actually, because I came joint second that year in the Sunday League six-hitters list, with eight. The two cricketers alongside me? Two other blockers: Roy Fredericks and John Shepherd! On a more serious note, 1973 also featured my highest first-class score, an innings of 215. It was made in early July, against Derbyshire at Derby, and when I found myself on 203 not out overnight I pleaded with Mike Denness, our captain, to let me bat on in the morning and not to declare immediately. The reason? My previous career-best was 203 against Cambridge University, and I didn't want that innings to stay in all the record books. I was going to end up with a career-best score of some kind, but I didn't want it to remain one which I had made against a university side! Fortunately, Mike listened to my begging - although I was still disappointed that Graham Johnson got out for 130 when our opening stand had reached 256, because that was then only 27 runs short of being a Kent first wicket record. That would have been worth having our names on, although the record has since passed to Mark Benson and Neil Taylor, who put on 300 at Canterbury in 1991.

I found myself acting as Kent's stand-in captain for a lot of the time in 1974, which was my first summer since 1969 that I did not play international cricket. Mike Denness was now England captain, having drawn his debut series 1-1 in the West Indies during the preceding winter, and I enjoyed the responsibility of being a senior player despite the usual, constant disruption of Test calls and injury. Besides the absences of Mike, Derek Underwood and Alan Knott on England duty,

Asif Iqbal disappeared off with the Pakistan tourists during the second half of the season and Bernard Julien was troubled by injury. But I batted consistently well all season, and indeed became the first player to score more than 1,000 runs in a season of domestic limited-overs cricket. I narrowly failed to score a hundred in all four competitions, my 97 against Derbyshire at Maidstone being my highest in the Sunday League. I also remember reaching 87 not out against Leicestershire in the first game of that John Player League season, when we won by nine wickets and I drove Ray Illingworth mad by continually making room to hit him away through the offside. Look at the Kent team, by the way, which thrashed Leicestershire on that May day: Luckhurst, Johnson, Denness, Asif, Ealham, Cowdrey, Knott, Shepherd, Julien, Woolmer, Underwood. There were eight Test players in the line-up plus a ninth soon to come in Bob Woolmer, five fully-fledged all-rounders plus Alan Knott, and ten players who could have been employed as front-line batsmen alone. Even 'Deadly' finished his career with a first-class hundred, too! When you glance back through the records and the scorecards, as I have done with great interest while compiling this book, it merely underlines what a privilege it was for all of us to have been involved in Kent's cricket history at this time.

Les Ames retired at the end of that 1974 season, meanwhile, fittingly after we had taken the Gillette Cup title again by beating Lancashire and avenging our 1971 defeat at Lord's. Les had given 50 years' service to Kent, as a player and administrator, and like myself now he was honoured by being appointed Kent president in the following year. When Les Ames spoke, everyone listened. He was respected by everyone at the club, both old and young, and he treated everyone the same. He could be forthright, but he said what he thought and it didn't matter to him whether he was chatting to the Queen or the local refuse collector. He had been highly successful as a player, both with Kent and England, and as an administrator he oversaw much change. As secretary-manager, he was highly influential in the growth of the great Kent team of the 1970's and he was never afraid to come into the dressing room - when he thought it appropriate - and voice his opinion. Les didn't believe in coaching, however, and thought that there were only two types of player: those that could play and those that couldn't.

My own belief is that there are those who need some coaching, and only a few who don't. I do believe that we have gone too far the other way now in English cricket, and that there are too many coaches around. Generally, I think we have gone a bit over the top in this area of the game. I am sure that a lot of my own contemporaries feel the same way about the general rise of the coach. Certainly, if you're a good enough player to play for England then I don't see the need for you then to be coached. Top players should have worked it out for themselves by then, and an experienced pair of eyes - to keep a check on them in case they fall back into bad habits - should be all that is required. At county level, I have an open mind about the need for specialist coaches. When I was the Kent coach I felt qualified and comfortable about giving batting coaching, but I always wanted to bring other specialists in on bowling. The sad thing these days, in the modern set-up, is that I am not qualified anymore to coach batting to under 18 year olds because I do not have the required badges.

Kent's glory years were based upon the talents of fine players, but also because people like Les Ames and Colin Page, who replaced Les as manager after 26 years' service of his own to the club, provided the continuity of expertise and planning which allowed that talent to develop and flourish. The great Kent team had character as well as talent, too, and a mix of personalities that provided added strength to the unit. People were encouraged to think for themselves, and take responsibility for their own actions both on and off the field. As with any good-sized group of people, there were occasional tensions, but professional sport is a precarious business at the best of times and I think we all understood each other well enough to put that all-important trust in our teammates.

I myself was about to take my leave of this great team, playing-wise at least, but the side kept on winning without me - with five more titles in the seasons of 1976, 1977 and 1978. Were they trying to tell me something? Seriously, my career-ending injury in the early summer of 1976 merely allowed Bob Woolmer the opportunity he had craved to open the batting - and, within a year, he was opening for England in Tests too.

Not that I knew it at the time, but at least I contributed as captain and batsman to a crucial victory at Sussex on May 22 which clinched our qualification from the Benson and Hedges Cup group. We needed to win to make sure it was us, and not Surrey, who scraped through in second position in the group - and, happily for us, Sussex themselves were out of contention for qualification. I called incorrectly at the toss but Tony Greig, the Sussex captain that day, surprisingly decided to bat first on what was a very green pitch. I was a relieved man to be able to walk back into our dressing room and announce that we would be bowling... everyone assumed I had won the toss! We bowled Sussex out for 85, with Bob Woolmer taking four wickets, Kevin Jarvis three and Asif Iqbal acting as our fifth bowler. Derek Underwood did not even get a bowl. I then finished up 65 not out, as we won by eight wickets, and it was to be the last man-of-the-match award of my career. Thanks, Greigy!

My fateful final finger injury came at Maidstone on Thursday June 3, when I was hit on the hand by the Northamptonshire and Pakistan pace bowler Sarfraz Nawaz. I had made 18 in Kent's second innings when Sarfraz made one seam back into me and lift. I got myself in a terrible position to play it, and the ball hit me on the back of the glove where there was no real protection. The result was that it knocked the top off the knuckle at the base of my right index finger, and made a bit of a mess. The real problem, though, was that the broken bone would just not set properly, and as a result it never really healed up as it should.

I attempted to get myself back into shape to play again before the end of the season, but there was never really a hope. Even before the injury, Colin Page had asked me to consider taking on the job of coaching and managing the second XI, and before the end of that summer I knew it was the right option at the right time for me. It would have been nice to have been able to say my farewells by playing in one last Canterbury Week, but it wasn't to be. I announced my retirement from first-class cricket at the end of a season in which we won both the Benson and Hedges Cup and the John Player League.

Chapter 9
Management

I think I could have played on at first-class level for a couple more seasons, certainly until I turned 40 in 1979, but it was right that I took the decision in 1976 to retire into the job of second team coach which the club had kindly offered to me. Yes, you are a long time retired, and I was still good enough to be playing for England in early 1975, but that job might not have been there for me if I had turned it down then... and, anyway, looking after the second team was an absolute joy.

My hand injury, sustained in the fourth championship fixture of the season, may have prevented me from achieving 1,000 runs for a 15th successive season, but my 14 on the trot is still a post-war county record that I can't see being broken now that there are fewer first-class games being played. Moreover, my time for scoring runs and getting records was very much over, and I relished the opportunity of helping to keep Kent's traditional supply of young talent coming through. Colin Page was in charge of the first team, and they were continuing to win trophies. I very much enjoyed the role of assisting him, once I had accepted the job on the terms that I would do it my way.

Colin was a different character to me, and his methods in and around the dressing room worked well for him. I realised, long before I even accepted his offer of the second team job, that I could not do it in a similar way - but Colin understood that as soon as I talked it over with him. He gave me his total support, and the four years I spent overseeing second team affairs are among the happiest of my cricketing life. I was just as capable of being firm or administering punishments or talking-to's, but I believed in doing that in private with the player concerned. I remember once, for instance, giving Neil Taylor the chance to offer his apology to the umpire for showing dissent on being given out in a second team game against Essex. We had a brief, but in my case straightforward, private chat - and I told him that he could either apologise or be left out by me for the following fortnight's cricket. Happily, Neil saw the sense in what I was talking and duly apologised during the next interval. With young players, all that kind of thing was part of the learning process, and I enjoyed being the person who was there to help them learn as much as to help them with the development of their game. After all, I had seen and experienced most things, from bagging a pair in both a second XI match and a Test match, and I could relate to everything they were going through.

I also had high hopes of some of the players in my charge at the end of the 1970's. The look of the first team was changing, with myself and Colin Cowdrey having retired and Mike Denness sadly falling out with the club and moving to Essex, but under Asif in 1977 and Alan Ealham in 1978 the success story stepped up a gear with two championship wins and, in 1978, the Benson and Hedges Cup again. Chris Tavare, Paul Downton, Chris Cowdrey, Kevin Jarvis and Graham Dilley were all coming through the ranks at this time, and it was exciting to see them fitting in so well alongside the more established stars that remained.

In fact, I would unhesitatingly say that I enjoyed my work with the second team far more than I did when I was involved for five subsequent seasons as first team manager.

Above: I am pictured captaining the Kent second XI during my spell as second team coach. Standing, on the far right, is future Kent captain Mark Benson

Left: England v Australia at Lord's, 1972. Walking out to bat with one of England's finest, Geoff Boycott

Colin Page's heart attack in early 1981 thrust me into doing a job at first team level that I was happy and willing enough to do... but it would have been better for all concerned if I had been left to continue my work with the seconds for a while longer.

As it was, Colin had to take a summer off in 1981 to get over his heart attack and John Pocock, who was then the club chairman, asked me to take over the first team as well as continue to oversee the seconds. I was grateful, that summer, for the help which David Nicholls gave me in terms of the second team - without his assistance, I could not have done both jobs to any level of satisfaction. As it was, it was a very tough summer indeed: I was often left trying to juggle several balls in the air at the same time, and that's difficult in any walk of life.

I'm afraid the situation also put a big strain on my relationship with Colin Page, for whom I had so much respect and to whom I owed so much. Colin was deemed fit enough to return to club duties later in 1981 but, for the following season, John Pocock informed me that he wanted the first team to remain under my management and that Colin should return to running the seconds. Colin, of course, wanted to be top man. He had earned that position by right, after all, and now it was being taken from him against his will. Yes, he had been told by the doctors to take things more steadily, but Colin still could not accept that he would not be in charge of the first eleven. I, of course, was caught in the middle and it was not pleasant. I made a point of telling Colin that it was not a case of me nicking his job. Indeed, I didn't really want his job at that time, because I was so happy myself with the seconds. It was a crying shame that me taking over from Colin did not happen naturally in that he was due for retirement anyway by the end of the 1980's and, by then, I would have served a proper 'apprenticeship' with the second XI.

What then happened, tragically, was that more ill health finally meant that Colin took early retirement in September 1990, having been Kent's director of youth coaching, and three months later he was dead when he suffered another heart attack while driving home from the Sevenoaks indoor cricket school. He pulled off the road into a lay-by when he felt unwell, and was later found dead in his car. Colin Page was a real one-off, as a character and a cricket man, and he did a brilliant job for Kent in an assocation with the club which lasted for 40 years.

My enjoyment in being second team coach was linked initially to the fact that I could operate so closely with the younger players. As Colin Page himself had done when I was coming up through the ranks, I actually played in the second XI matches too. I only batted as a tailender, of course, and only bowled very occasionally, but in 1977 it is pleasing to report that I topped both the batting and bowling averages for Kent seconds! My 13 innings brought no fewer than nine not outs and 315 runs, and 18.1 overs of by now very creaky left-arm spin resulted in seven wickets for just 32 runs!

The serious point about this, though, is that I was in the position of being able to show the youngsters the value of certain attributes and certain approaches while actually being out there with them, and I found this very rewarding. I also made it part of my job to throw myself wholeheartedly into the fielding drills and practices, and I couldn't understand the attitude of some of my fellow county second XI coaches - such as, I remember, Peter Sainsbury of Hampshire - who preferred to sit on the sidelines during play. If I was capable of doing it, I wanted to show all the youngsters that I was just as keen to improve and to work as I hoped they were.

When you look at young cricketers, you have in my view to look at the whole package. Ability, yes, but also their character and their ability to learn. And, most importantly, how much they want it. Improving as a cricketer, in order to get to first-class level, is all about watching and learning and working. Hard work is needed, too, and batsmen like Neil Taylor and Mark Benson were classic examples of lads who worked very hard for what they achieved in the game, which in the end was considerable and deserved to be rewarded by more than just the single Test cap they got between them. I felt a great deal of pleasure, in subsequent years, from seeing players like Neil and Mark get their first hundred, or score their first 1,000 runs in a season, because I had worked hard alongside them to get their games right. Mark Benson, for example, had a big tendency to fall over to the offside when he came to Kent from Sutton Valence School, and we worked for hour upon hour to correct this flaw. It was something, in fact, that he always had to be aware of during his career, but in the end he became one of the very best leavers of a ball that I have ever seen - and that was all down to the work he put in to understand his own game and act upon it. It gave me as much of a thrill as it gave all those players, to be honest, whenever they were successful.

It was fascinating for me, too, to see how certain players fell away despite having huge amounts of natural talent - Nick Kemp, for example, was an all-rounder with as much going for him cricket-wise as Chris Cowdrey, but unlike Chris he just couldn't put it all together when he got out into the middle. Then there were lads who became very friendly and in effect helped to give each other the confidence to express themselves on the field. Outsiders, especially, must have thought it strange that two youngsters like Guy Spelman, a former Sevenoaks School head boy, and Graham Dilley, who came from a Dartford comprehensive and had a completely different background, became the best of pals. But they were both fast bowlers and cricket gave them a common bond which led to a great friendship.

Dealing with different personalities, at an age when young lads are sometimes trying to make statements about themselves and doing a lot of growing up, was another big aspect of the second team job which I enjoyed. I remember when Richard Ellison, another very talented young player of course, came to play his first game for the second XI. At lunchtime he really tucked in to the boiled potatoes and had a huge number of them piled high on top of his salad. Suddenly, he caught my eye, and looked down at his plate. "Sorry," he said, "I wasn't sure how many to take." And then he started to put back most of them into the bowl in the middle of the table! Elly always loved his food, but he had to learn to be just a bit less enthusiastic about it during matches!

Then there was Derek Aslett, a fine young batsman from Dover who also went on to have a successful first team career but who in those early days used to turn out for Kent seconds when he came back from summer term at Leicester University. He was going through a rebellious stage, one year, and he devised a way of flaunting the dress code at the club which required you to turn up for matches in a smart pair of trousers. He used to drive down from his flat in Blackheath in his favourite jeans, and then pull his other trousers over the top of them literally just before entering the ground. But it backfired on him one day at Chelmsford when he had been rostered to look after the medical box. He then happened to be out in the middle batting when we in the dressing room needed it for something. I called out to him at the end of an over to ask where it was and he called back: "It's in the car - my keys are in my trouser pocket." Of course, when I went to find the keys they were inside the pockets of his jeans which were hung up on a hook inside the other pair of trousers. He had taken both off at the same time, in order to keep the jeans hidden from view, but as a result of being rumbled he was duly fined double for cheating! It gave everyone a bit of a laugh, too, and Derek took it very well.

Steve Marsh was another young lad who came into the second team environment during that time, and we have often chuckled since about what happened on his first appearance. I had received a letter from George Baker at The Mote Cricket Club, telling me about this youngster who they felt could get a good deal better. In those days, in addition to the regular midweek second XI matches, I used to run a Sunday colts team that had fixtures against the Kent League clubs, which was specifically designed to give up-and-coming players a chance to impress. So I arranged for young S A Marsh to play in a match against Ashford. He kept wicket very well, but at that stage did not have much of a reputation with the bat and so was down to come in at number 10, just before me at number 11. Eventually, when he was due to go in, we still needed 35 to win with only about three overs remaining. I pulled him to one side and quickly said: "Steve, we can't win this game now - but I don't want to lose it. Understand?" He nodded, and strode in. He then attempted to play every shot in the book to the deliveries he faced, connecting on only a few occasions, and we finished well short of the target. On his return to the dressing room, I again asked him for a quiet word and said: "Did we not talk about what the tactics were before you went out?" He replied: "Yes, you said to block it out, but I thought we could still win it." "Listen," I told him, "One day, if you are the captain, you can make those decisions - but, at the moment, it's me, and you didn't carry out the orders that were given to you." It was a telling-off, but at the same time it showed me that here was an 18-year old with terrific self-confidence. What you don't want is for confidence to become arrogance, and in Steve's case I'm happy to say that he was never arrogant. On that first meeting with him, I didn't want to kill his enthusiasm and competitive streak, but I needed to remind him very early that he wasn't yet in a position to make those sorts of decisions. His self-belief, though, contributed to his becoming both a very fine player and a strong-minded Kent captain. His batting also improved enormously and he could - and in my view should - have played for England.

The only downside, for me, of being involved with young players was when you had to tell someone who was desperate to become a county cricketer that they were not good enough. It was awful being the one to tell someone like young David Riley, a leg-spinner who had come down from Yorkshire, that he was not being kept on. There were often tears, and it was always a very difficult thing to do with those young lads - like David, for instance - who had given you and his own cricket 100 per cent. I didn't mind so much having to tell those who had not put in the work, although it was still hard to see a talented young player not achieve what he desired. Yet at least I knew what it all meant to them - I had been in their shoes once myself, and I knew too how close I had once come to being released.

Judging a cricketer takes experience, and a good eye for the little things as much as the obvious ability. There are times when someone looks very special, but doesn't make it, and other times when someone seems unexceptional but earns himself a long professional career through sheer hard work and character. The telling time, for me, is always out there in the middle. It's not about how good or bad someone looks in the nets. It's about whether you can achieve, and not about looking the part. And I also always keep an open mind about lads, because they can change so much from 14 to 16 to 18. I like to encourage them to express their views about cricket, too, because I'm not the gospel and because I want cricketers who think and talk about the game naturally. I didn't want robots. Overall, and I'm sure that this applies to all professional sport and not just cricket, ability is less than 50 per cent of what you need to be successful.

The start of my five seasons in charge of the Kent first team coincided with the beginning of a period of further change. There were times, initially, when I found it a

bit awkward with senior players around like Graham Johnson, Derek Underwood, Alan Knott, Asif Iqbal and Bob Woolmer. These were great friends of mine, first and foremost, but now I was being paid to take an overview of the team situation and to make decisions for the good of the whole and not for any particular individuals.
I had to be a little bit separate from the players, in other words, and that is not an easy thing to do when you are very close to them as a former teammate. It was another reason why it would have been better for me to have had more years solely in charge of the seconds before moving up to the first team.

Nevertheless, I did enjoy too this part of my time at Kent, and I don't think we did badly on the field from 1981-85, despite the lack of a trophy. Under Chris Tavare's captaincy, in particular, we reached the Nat West Trophy final at Lord's for two years in succession - losing by 24 runs to Somerset in 1983 and then in the last over by four wickets against Middlesex 12 months later. We also finished seventh and fifth in the championship in those same two seasons, and there was a third place in the John Player League in 1983 and a fourth place the previous year.

Chris Tavare had taken over the captaincy for the 1983 season, after I had been asked in 1982 to give both him and Chris Cowdrey the chance to lead the side before it was decided who should take over full-time from Asif Iqbal. At the end of that summer I was invited to appear in front of Kent's 22-man general committee and instructed to make my recommendation. After speaking for five or ten minutes about the respective abilities of the two prospective leaders I said that, having played alongside his father for more than a dozen years, it would be a great pleasure for me to recommend Chris Cowdrey.....but that I couldn't do that. Chris Tavare was my recommendation to be captain, and he was duly elected in a 12-10 vote.

There remained, however, a significant amount of support behind the scenes for Chris Cowdrey, even though to my mind Chris Tavare was doing a fine job.
Two years later, totally against my wishes, it was decided by the committee that a change of captaincy was needed. What is more, when I made a point of asking about the time of the meeting which I knew was going to decide this issue, I was told that my presence there would not be required.

It really hurt me that I was not allowed to attend that meeting, yet I knew that even if I had defiantly turned up to argue the case from my point of view, I would have simply been asked to leave. And, by then, I also knew that if I had threatened to resign if Chris Tavare was replaced it would not have made any difference.
There had been no attempt by Chris Cowdrey, either, to undermine the captain - it was completely a committee decision. Chris Tavare stayed on to play under Chris Cowdrey because he had a benefit season scheduled for 1988, but left for Somerset in 1989.

I was relieved of the job of cricket manager at the end of the 1985 season, but what Kent didn't have to do, though, was find another role for me within the club, and I was grateful to hear that I was being offered a new job in the administrative department. The bottom line for me was that I didn't want to leave Kent, despite everything that had happened in the previous 12 months, and many years of playing and then managing left me more than qualified to do the administrative work that was now being offered up. I was doing things like arranging new contracts, dealing with all the players on day-to-day matters, and organising travel and accommodation for each of the club's teams. Being away from the daily cut-and-thrust of the dressing room front line was something I immediately missed, but at the age of 46 I was more than happy to take on my new backseat role. I was, after all, still at Kent and I was still involved.

Chapter 10

Man of Kent

Jim Swanton once popped in to see me during my 10 years as manager of the Ames-Levett Sports Centre at the St Lawrence Ground and said, in that naturally authoritative manner of his: "Brian, you may be interested to know that there is a coaching job going up at Lord's... and, if you apply, I understand that you might well get it." Well, that was very nice of Jim to tip me the wink but do you know my reply? "Thanks, Jim," I said, "but why would I want to leave Kent? I'm a Kent boy, so why would I want to go all the way to Lord's to work?" I think he understood the reasons why I would dismiss that sort of opportunity so readily, and I don't regret doing so. Perhaps he thought, with my experience in the game, I should be more involved in cricket and with cricketers than I was by that time, but in truth I was where I wanted to be... at Canterbury.

As manager of the sports centre, I had a small office with a balcony on the top floor which looked out over the whole expanse of the St Lawrence Ground. The famous lime tree was directly opposite me over the other side of the playing area, and on match days I often used to treat myself at around 5.30pm (the end of my working day at the sports centre) by grabbing a beer and retiring to the balcony to watch the last hour or so's cricket. Sometimes a few people would join me, and on occasions the balcony was also used as an extra facility for some corporate guests, but there were also times when I was able to sit there on my own and just drink in the atmosphere of what is such a wonderful setting for cricket. Why, indeed, I used to think, would I want to be anywhere else?

How I came to be the sports centre manager, however, is another part of my Kent story which, when you look back, rather defies belief. It all happened in October 1990. The club had lost money that year, and it was rumoured that there would not be the finance available to appoint anyone in what was intended to be a new position of sports centre manager. The centre was being built, at a cost of £450,000, and needed someone to run it, so I went home one evening and, after a bit too much red wine and a long discussion with my wife, I decided to knock on the secretary Stuart Anderson's door the next morning and offer myself as an existing, internal candidate for the job. By this time I felt that much of my administrative work could be handled by others, and to be honest I fancied the new challenge that such a role would bring. To my surprise, really, following a committee meeting, the club agreed that I should take it on, and it was the beginning of another chapter in my employment at Kent County Cricket Club.

I had no experience at all of running a sports centre, of course, but I was determined to learn as fast as I could. These days, you would need to take a three or four-year course to get the necessary qualifications, but I did not have that luxury. Instead, I immediately arranged to visit three local sports centres in east Kent - at the University of Kent, in Dover, and in Folkestone. I knew all three of the managers well, and I spent the best part of a day with each of them asking questions about how their particular sports centres were run. I am very grateful to Mike Wilkins at the University of Kent, Dave Scoggins at the Dover Sports

Above: I am honoured to have a part of the St Lawrence Ground at Canterbury named after me. And it is even better that cricket lovers can go to 'my' bar in the Ames-Levett Cricket School to chat about the game

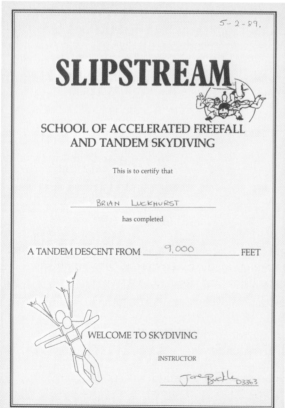

5-2-89.

SLIPSTREAM

SCHOOL OF ACCELERATED FREEFALL AND TANDEM SKYDIVING

This is to certify that

BRIAN LUCKHURST

has completed

A TANDEM DESCENT FROM _____ 9,000 _____ FEET

WELCOME TO SKYDIVING

INSTRUCTOR

Left: This is nothing to do with my 50 years at Kent, but it took a bit of doing so I am going to include it in my book! As a surprise 50th birthday present, from my wife Raye, I did my one and only parachute jump in the skies above Headcorn

Centre, and Derek Searle at Folkestone who showed me around and explained their management roles in detail. Indeed, the advice I received from those three gentlemen shaped how I approached my new job at Kent's facility. Their help was crucial, because cricket-based sports centres in those days were mainly loss leaders. I understand that, in the whole of the country at that time, there was only one which made a profit.

When I started as sports centre manager in January 1991 my brief from Kent was to try to break even, and I soon realised that to do so I needed to get a lot more people in to use it. I devised a monthly booking sheet, for the next 12 months, so that we could try to plan ahead more and attract future business. But I remember that when we reached the end of February I looked ahead on the booking sheet and saw, in particular, that May had no bookings whatsoever! Alarm bells began to ring.

My daily ritual, now, was to be there (on my own) every morning and evening, and have an afternoon break in which I often tried to get home for a meal. But I knew that I had to attract more business urgently, because the centre could not break even on cricket coaching sessions and winter practice nights for local cricket clubs. For a start, I contacted the Kent County Football Association and - with their blessing - I wrote to 200 local soccer clubs telling them I intended to run a summer indoor football league. The result was leagues which ran for four nights a week, all summer, and with the help of Don and Margaret Anstead I was also able to initiate a regular Monday night netball league. We managed to get badminton started, too, and I wrote to local schools knowing that day-time bookings from them would be vital to maximising the overall use of the facility.

As a result of much hard work, the sports centre always made a profit - even in that first year. Over my 10 years in charge, moreover, the Ames-Levett Centre made a total profit of around £150,000. It was a little bit better than breaking even, and I'm very proud of that achievement and the way that we were able to expand the facility in terms of its business success. An extension was built four years into my management time, which enabled us to add on and run a fitness suite and to have a restaurant, balcony and second bar. This £250,000 development meant, for me, that I had to learn more new skills. I had never worked behind a bar before I took over the sports centre management, never run a till, and never changed beer barrels or things like that. The first thing I did when I went in every morning was to sweep the floor and tidy and clean, but now I had to learn how to manage functions too in the new Seventies Room restaurant and bar.

I used to work 80-hour weeks when it first opened, and after a while the club suggested that I should slow down and I was given a part-time helper. Soon, he became a full-time colleague and, these days, the sports centre employs three full-time staff and a number of part-timers too. I am delighted that it has become a valuable and valued part of the scenery at the St Lawrence Ground and so pleased, as you can imagine, that the Kent club decided to name the main bar there as Lucky's Bar, in my honour. Towards the end of my spell in charge there, I was also joined at work by my wife Raye, because she took on the catering franchise and provided all the food for the functions which took place in the Seventies Room. I'm told the food there and in Lucky's Bar was some of the finest on the ground!

After a decade as sports centre manager, and 46 years in Kent's employment, I moved back into the office in the year 2000 after accepting an invitation to work a three-day week in the club's commercial department. To be able to complete my 50 years at Kent by working alongside people like Jon Fordham and Jean Owens was a real pleasure, and I hope I made a contribution to the way Kent cricket has been so well marketed in recent times. My long involvement with the club did help me to open some doors, and to get to use my name to help to sell Kent cricket was a great way for me to finish my fifth decade at Canterbury.

As a player you are on one side of the fence at a county club and, as an administrator, you are on the other side. That's the way it inevitably has to be, but I believe that both parts of the club can do much to understand and appreciate the other. As a former player myself, I made it my business to tell Matthew Fleming and David Fulton, our captains of the past few years, that I would be delighted to help out in any way I could to make all the players feel more a part of the whole club. Both Matthew and David have done well in stressing to the players the importance of supporting the commercial initiatives. And, after working in the marketing department for my last four years as an employee, I certainly understand better than I ever did how vital commercial success is. In fact, without a successful marketing side there would be no club. It is as simple as that.

I have a picture at home of myself and Mike Denness walking out to bat at Canterbury in our 1967 Gillette Cup semi-final against Sussex. You are struck by the enormous crowd packed into the ground, but I am also struck these days by the complete and utter absence of any advertisement boards. We are, indeed, in a different era now and the way Kent cricket can sell its product to the outside world underpins everything that we hold so dear.

My time at the sports centre and in Jon Fordham's commercial department, in which my official title was business development manager, enabled me to learn so much more about the day-to-day realities of how a modern sporting business is run. In retirement, starting of course with my year as club president, I want to continue to make a contribution by putting all my 50-year experience towards trying to make Kent County Cricket Club the best it can be.

There is one legacy of my last decade and a half at Canterbury, however, which gives me enormous personal pleasure - and which I very much hope outlasts me too. During the last few years, while walking around the St Lawrence Ground on match days, I've sometimes overheard spectators in conversation about where to meet later. And, in many cases, they say things like: "I'll see you up in Lucky's Bar", or "What about a pint in Lucky's Bar?" Colin Cowdrey, Frank Woolley and Les Ames may have stands named after them at Canterbury, but I've got a bar full of people talking about the cricket and having a good time… and that will do me very nicely!

A fine body of men: the Kent over 50's team which won the national knockout title in 1989. The side also won the competition in 1991. Carl Openshaw, the current Kent chairman, captained the team and is pictured in the middle of the front row

A fine body of young men: a Kent under 10's team is photographed with their guest for the day

Chapter 11
True Greats

The story of my 50 years at Kent is, of course, interwoven with so many of the great names in the club's history. I have written about a great number of them in the preceding pages, but I also wanted this book to record the selection I made in March 2003, before the start of my final summer as an employee of Kent County Cricket Club, of the greatest post-War XI that - in a fantasy match - could have been put into the field.

The following is a reproduction of the five articles I wrote for the Kent on Sunday newspaper, which appeared in print on five successive weekends and which gradually built up into my finally revealed XI. Actually, it ended up as a XII, but the reasons for that will be quite apparent as you read on!

I broke my selected Kent team into five separate units: two opening batsmen, three specialist middle-order batsmen, an all-rounder and wicket-keeper, two spinners, and two fast bowlers.

Here are my deliberations and, at the end of it, what a team it is…

The Opening Batsmen

The first big decision I had to make, when considering the options as to who would open the batting in my best post-1945 Kent XI, was what to do about myself!

I played 21 Test matches for England, from 1970 to 1974, and also scored 39 hundreds for Kent. My 389-match first-class career, from my Kent debut in 1958 to my out-of-retirement one-off game against the 1985 Australians, brought me 22,303 runs at an average of 38.12 and included 48 centuries. But I was not good enough to get into this team.

Nor is my old opening partner and great friend Mike Denness, who went on to captain England of course, and nor is Arthur Fagg, who scored more than 26,000 runs and hit 55 hundreds for Kent between 1932 and 1957. Bob Wilson's 19,458 county runs, from 1952-67, do not get him selection for this side, and neither does Peter Richardson - another former England opener like Fagg and myself.

My choices to go in first are Mark Benson and Neil Taylor, whose Kent careers ran almost side-by-side for 16 seasons or so until 1995, and it gives me enormous pleasure to name them as my best Kent opening batsmen since the War because I was one of those involved in the coaching that both received as they came up from the junior ranks in the late 1970's and into the early 1980's.

Looking back, it still seems criminal to me that Mark won just a single Test cap (against India in 1986) and Neil did not win even one. Both of them were good enough to have had lengthy England careers, and their quality as batsmen is underlined by their respective records.

Benson scored 18,284 runs for Kent at an average of 40.27. Only three other players, with more than 10,000 runs to their name, have averaged over 40 for the county - and those three are Frank Woolley, Les Ames and Colin Cowdrey. 'Benny' is thus in the very highest company, while Neil would also have been in this exclusive club had his last innings for Kent in 1995 been a hundred (he scored 5 & 8 against Derbyshire in his last first-class match for the county before leaving to go to Sussex a year later).

Taylor's county record is 17,721 runs at 39.82, and he scored 42 Kent hundreds compared to Benson's 48. What gets them both into this team, however, besides their ability, is their powers of concentration.

All openers get their fair share of low scores, because that is an occupational hazard when you bat against the new ball. But, if you get in, then it is your job to occupy the crease. That is what Benson and Taylor could both do exceptionally well - and it is something which Rob Key, to give a modern example, must learn to do more consistently.

Key, actually, has enough natural talent to become the very best Kent opener of all time. I was asked several years ago to do 10 one-on-one coaching sessions with Robert at Canterbury. After five of them, I told him that if I had possessed the same potential at his age (he was then 20) I would have won 100 caps for England, and not 21. In the next few seasons we will be seeing exactly how good Rob Key can become.

But back to Benson and Taylor. As a left-and-right handed combination, and well-used to batting together, they will provide the perfect base-work for the innings. Their running between the wickets, and general judge of a run, might not have been as good as the understanding Mike Denness and I had, but it was solid and - technically - both were as good, if not better, than Mike and I. It is their ability to occupy the crease which gives them my nod.

Neil Taylor was also a fine player of really fast bowling. He and Mark both had a great temperament, and in a different era both would have been capped many times. Temperament, and having the right attitude and desire to do well, is in my eyes at least 50 per cent of what is required to be a top player. Ability is no more than 50 per cent. Someone like Trevor Ward, for instance, who scored almost 12,000 runs for Kent at an average of 35, could have been an even better player if he had possessed a better temperament. In-form, he was a wonderful entertainer.

Benson had a great eye, too, so good that he perfected the knack of withdrawing the bat so late that many observers and commentators thought he had played and missed. But there was a rumour, after he had been dropped following his one Test appearance, in which he scored 21 and 30 by the way, that Mark couldn't play spin. What rubbish!

I played 21 Tests, from the age of 31, because I was lucky. Colin Milburn lost an eye in a car accident during the summer of 1969 and, because of that, I got my chance as an England player. I scored a hundred in my second Test match, and I then got a good run in the side.

Mark and Neil were not so fortunate, mainly I suppose because of the presence of Graham Gooch as an automatic selection in the England sides of their era, but both were very fine players indeed and great products of the Kent system.

The Middle-Order

In all my long association with the game I love, there is one man who stands out head and shoulders above the rest I have played with in terms of natural talent - and that is the man I always called 'The Master'.

Colin Cowdrey had so much ability as a batsman that he could have played for England without having had a single coaching session in his life. In fact, if he had

Les Ames, in full flow. He is the only wicketkeeper-batsman to score more than a hundred hundreds in first-class cricket

Arthur Fagg, the former Kent opener who remains the only man in cricket history to score two double hundreds in the same match

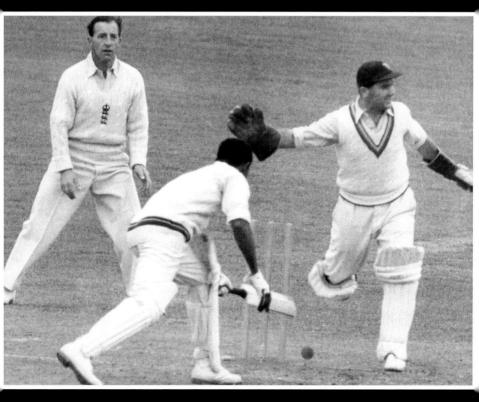

Another victim for the incomparable Godfrey Evans. Standing at first slip is Bill Edrich

possessed more belief in himself he would have been the best player of his generation in the world - he was that good.

He was a brilliant all-round games player, in fact, and was both squash and rackets champion of Tonbridge School as well as first appearing for the first XI at cricket when he was just 13.

In 114 Tests he scored 7,624 runs for England, at an average of 44, with 22 hundreds. In all first-class cricket, it was 42,719 with 107 centuries - and 58 of those were for Kent.

Yet, I can remember an incident quite late in his career which summed up the lack of self-belief which went with his incredible ability. We were playing a match at Canterbury, and Colin had got a bit stuck on 98 first-class hundreds. He had got out a couple of times in the 70's in previous games, and after his dismissal for a lowish score in this particular match he went for a long soak in the bath.

I just happened to be walking past, in the corridor outside, and I realised that Colin was nearly in tears. He was sat in the bath, with no-one else around. I went in and said 'Come on, Master', but he replied that he didn't think he was going to be able to get to his 100th hundred. Of course, I just told him that he would, and it was certainly no surprise to me that he reached that landmark a few weeks later at Maidstone.

But how could anyone with 98 hundreds and his record have been that worried about his form? Well, that was Colin. Even when he played for England and batted with Peter May it was interesting how Peter used to annihilate the bowling when he was on top but Colin, when in prime form, just caressed the ball around.

He was such a lovely man, too, and when he was knighted I started to call him 'Sir Master'. But when he became Lord Cowdrey I asked him what I should call him then. Colin replied 'I suppose it should be My Lord and Master!'

My initial feeling, when picking this side of mine, was to have Cowdrey at number three and to follow him with Asif Iqbal at four and Les Ames at five. Asif was, like Colin, a superb natural games player but, unlike 'The Master', he had all the self-belief and self-confidence in the world. He was a wonderful man to have on your side, and in your dressing room, and although he came to Kent as an overseas player I tend to think of him as one of 'ours'.

I have not considered most overseas players for this particular exercise, by the way, because players like Rahul Dravid, Aravinda de Silva, Steve Waugh and Carl Hooper would otherwise pack the team and turn it into merely an International XI. But Asif gets in because he was not a short-term employee and because he became part of the Kent scenery between 1968, when he arrived from Pakistan more as a whippy medium-paced swing bowler who batted, and his last county season in 1982. He also scored 26 hundreds for Kent, and averaged 37, despite having the worst stance and grip on the bat that I have ever seen! It worked for him, though, and he was just the sort of cricketer who underlined the adage that cricket coaches should never try to change people who have a natural talent but an unorthodox method.

Les Ames played his last match for Kent in 1951, so technically he qualifies for this team. But most of his great career was played out before the War, when he won all his 47 Test caps, so I would like to have Les on board as team manager!

He would simply have to be around in some capacity, because no-one has done more for Kent cricket than Les Ames. He scored 78 hundreds for Kent, and eight for England - for whom he mainly played as a wicketkeeper-batsman. By the time I made my Kent debut in 1958 Les was in charge of things off the field and he,

Colin Cowdrey and Colin Page provided the brilliant manager/captain/coach partnership that was to shape the great Kent team of the 1970's.

If I cannot have Les, then, I will go for Chris Tavare as my final pick in the middle-order. And, moreover, I will bat Chris at three, so that Colin moves down to four and Asif comes in with even more licence to entertain at number five. Tavare hit 29 centuries for Kent, before leaving the county for Somerset in late 1988, and his 14,201 county runs came at a whisker under 38 per innings. He was a marvellous strokemaker in the middle-order, before England asked him to open and his technique became more defensive. But that was Tav - doing what the team needed without question because England needed a replacement for Geoff Boycott at the head of the order.

In fact, Chris would have been a good captain of England besides being a fine leader at Kent in the 1983 and 1984 seasons. He was softly-spoken and undemonstrative, and virtually whispered in team talks, but everyone listened. He also never panicked on the field, and was a great catcher at slip.

The Kent committee, however, decided to replace him as captain with Chris Cowdrey after just two years at the helm. Cowdrey had not touted himself for the job, and yet the committee decided to replace Tavare. It was against my wishes as the team manager at the time and, in my view, it was without doubt the worst decision that the county has made since the War.

The All-Rounder and Wicket-Keeper

One of the greatest traditions in English cricket is the Kentish tradition of producing superb wicket-keepers. While Nottinghamshire or Derbyshire could always seem to whistle up a fast bowler from the nearest coal-mine, Kent have enjoyed a rich seam of world-class stumpers.

In the early part of the last century it was Fred Huish, who still holds most Kent records for wicketkeeping, and then came Les Ames, who claimed 842 dismissals in his 430 matches for the county. Since the War, however, and for the purposes of this task of mine, I have to make a choice between two truly great England wicket-keepers - while giving honourable mentions to both Steve Marsh and Paul Downton, a proud Kent lad who had to move to Middlesex to forge a first-class career which led to 30 England caps.

The reason Downton left Kent was simple - Alan Knott, who was then still at the height of his considerable powers and an absolute genius behind the stumps. Knotty, however, faces stiff competition for a place in this post-1945 Kent side from another unique talent in Godfrey Evans. 'Godders' played in 91 Tests for England - in an era when our national side was arguably the strongest it has ever been - while Knott appeared in 95 Tests. What a choice to have to make!

In the end, though, I must go with Knott. Look at his figures. He claimed 915 dismissals in the 349 first-class matches he played for Kent between 1964 and 1985, and also scored 11,339 runs at an average of 27.58. Marsh, by the way, also topped 10,000 Kent runs, and averaged 28, which underlines just what a fine cricketer he was - but he was another player (like Neil Taylor in this side) who did not get an England chance despite having a great county record.

Knott, meanwhile, scored 4,389 Test runs at an average of 32.75, with five centuries, which confirms his status as a world-class all-rounder. Evans could be distinctly useful with the bat, but Knott was as good a keeper - in my view - besides being a wonderfully unorthodox but highly effective batsman.

"We're preparing it for Colin Cowdrey"

www.thisislondon.com/blower

Above: This is the cartoon, by Blower in the London Evening Standard, which was published following Colin Cowdrey's death in December 2000. It says it all

Left: Former Kent and England fast bowler Fred Ridgway

Godfrey's reputation was built around his magnificent ability standing up to the stumps, even to bowlers of fastish-medium, but he was a showman at heart while Knotty played the odds more carefully. Knott reckoned that, yes, he might bring off a couple of extra stumpings by standing up to some of the quicker bowlers, but that he might then miss around 10 catches in the process. There is no doubt that Alan could have done everything, technically, that Godfrey did, but he chose not to in the wider interests of the team.

What is amazing to recall, now, is that Knotty actually joined the Kent staff as an off-spinner! But it was when he showed off his wicket-keeping skills that the county knew that they had found the long-term successor to Godfrey.

Of course, Knott's partnership and almost telepathic understanding with Derek Underwood - both with Kent and England - has already reached a mythical level. And it was quite extraordinary, I can tell you, having spent quite a lot of my own career watching with pleasure their double act at close quarters.

Underwood, who bowled his left-arm spinners and cutters pretty quickly anyway, also possessed a much quicker delivery which we all knew as the Exocet Ball. Well, Knotty knew from the first step of Derek's approach when the Exocet was coming - and it must have been around 80 miles per hour, at least, compared to the bowling speeds that I now see revealed by television's speed-gun technology. I remember one particular leg-side stumping he pulled off, from Derek's quicker ball, to dismiss Roger Prideaux of Northamptonshire. It was an astonishing feat of reflexes and skill - and I have so many memories to cherish of Knotty pulling off dismissals like that.

He is also the loveliest of men, if completely different from anyone else! He still loves his honey, and his attention to detail in terms of cricket-preparation and diet was remarkable, if more than a little mad! Who can forget all his constant on-field stretching, and exercising, for instance?

Knotty never missed a game, mind, although he always thought he might have something wrong with him. On England tours he used to go and see Bernard Thomas, the physio, almost every morning with some little ache or pain he wanted him to check out!

I also recall him rejecting 10 different pairs of gloves that his sponsor Slazenger had sent him before he found a pair that he liked, and his Mum used to keep repairing his floppy white sun hat so that he didn't have to buy a new one. Superstition? Yes, I think so.

As a cricketer, though, he was magnificent and his batting style was the result of countless experiments in the nets and many hours spent thinking about what would work for him. He was also a nightmare to bowl to, as he used to do all the things that you are not supposed to - like hitting leg-spinners through mid-wicket and off-spinners over extra cover. Yet if he had been a batsmen only, and not a wicket-keeper, I believe he could have held down a job as a number five in county cricket.

In this side, however, he is down to go in at number seven because I am picking my all-rounder - Bob Woolmer - to go in at number six. Bob was a quality batsman, good enough to be reckoned England's best in terms of technique by the time he opted to join Kerry Packer's World Series Cricket in 1977 and deny himself many more than his eventual 19 Test caps.

He came to Kent, though, as a medium-paced swing bowler and it is incredible to look back at something like the 1973 Benson and Hedges Cup final and see him batting at number nine! Yet the strength of the Kent team in those days meant that Bob, despite the obvious batting ability which was to bring him 12,634 county runs at 35.09 and 28 hundreds, had to wait for the chance to go up the order. His bowling, too, was good enough in his early years for him to be chosen on that alone, and he could swing the ball both ways at a similar pace to, say, Mark Ealham.

Ealham junior, by the way, gets into the frame for my all-rounder's position, and his eight Test caps and 64 one-day international appearances will bear future testimony to the quality of his all-round cricket. Mark is so like his father Alan - both love to give the ball a biff, both are fantastic fielders and both are huge eaters! Mark, though, can bowl a bit too, which his old man couldn't do!

Graham Johnson was another great Kent all-rounder, scoring 12,509 first-class runs and taking 560 wickets with his greatly-underrated off-spin from 1965-85, besides being another fine fielder and an integral part of the great 70's team.

Before Graham, there was also Alan Dixon, who was the sort of cricketer who could do everything. He was a marvellous cover fielder, a great striker of the ball in the lower-middle order and a talented medium-paced bowler who could also change style and bowl effective off-breaks.

But Bob Woolmer gets my vote, for the class of his batting and his ability as a bowler to take vital wickets and get good batsmen out - like when he bowled New Zealand Test opener Glenn Turner through the gate to help to set up our 1973 B&H Cup final victory. Woolmer was the best player of fast bowling in a great Kent team, and he modelled himself on his hero Colin Cowdrey. The best compliment I can pay Bob is that, technically and style-wise, he was the nearest thing to Colin that I have seen.

The Spinners

When I turned my attention to picking two spinners for this team I was only grateful that I had been given two choices! To have had to leave out either Doug Wright or Derek Underwood would have been dreadful.

Kent supporters were fortunate indeed, between 1932 and 1987, to have had only five seasons (outside of the War years) when there wasn't a Wright or an Underwood to terrorise opposition batsmen: Doug's last appearance was in 1957 and Derek made his first-class debut as a 17-year old in 1963 - a summer in which he took 101 wickets at 21.12!

To call both men 'slow' bowlers is almost an insult, however. Both sent the ball down with a real fizz, but it might be eye-opening to the younger generation of Kent fans for me to confirm that leg-spinner Wright was actually a good deal quicker through the air, and off the pitch, than Underwood.

Yet 'Deadly Derek' was not exactly slow! In last week's article I said that Underwood's famed Exocet Ball would have been measured at around 80 miles per hour if today's speed-gun technology had been available when he was in his prime. But Doug Wright's normal pace was quicker than Derek's and his own faster ball was also in excess of 80 mph.

Wright also made his county debut at 17, and in fact was 17 days younger than Underwood was on his own first-class bow 31 years later. But it should be of no surprise that both were youthful prodigies, because both were 'one-offs' in terms of their ability and bowling style.

Underwood's left-arm spinners and cutters were highly rhythmical and stunningly consistent. He didn't mind batsmen trying to hit him over the top, and sometimes succeeding, because he knew he'd then have a better chance of getting them out. But what Derek hated was bowling a bad delivery and making life easy for his opponent. He used to get so cross with himself for bowling even one bad ball!

Wright ran in even further than Underwood - in fact, he used to bound in off 15 paces and even at the pace he bowled he could deliver a genuine googly or flipper to supplement his leg-breaks and top-spinners. He was a freak, in a way. It is still a disappointment to me that I never faced him during his county years, even though I was on the Kent staff during his last few seasons. But we juniors used not to be allowed to bat against the first team bowlers in those days - we were there simply to bowl at the first team batsmen!

But, when I was in my best years as a batsman around 1970, I remember coming up against Doug in a benefit match being played at Highland Court. He must have been well into his 50's by this stage, and as I walked out to bat he said to me from the end of his run-up that he was sorry, but he wouldn't be giving me one off the mark! What happened? Well, it only lasted a few balls, but I was soon walking back to the pavilion, lbw for 0, and I can tell you that Doug was a pretty useful bowler even then. In his pomp, he must have been a fearsome proposition.

Wright, indeed, took 1709 wickets for Kent in 397 first-class matches, plus 108 in his 34 Tests for England. He also took a world-record seven hat-tricks in first-class cricket, and was on a hat-trick another 15 times! That just shows how difficult he was to counter, especially when you first went in. He finished with five wickets or more in an innings on no fewer than 132 occasions for the county - which was five more times than Underwood, despite 'Deadly' playing in 123 more first-class matches for Kent!

I can remember a match at Maidstone in 1956, against Middlesex, when Doug took 8-30 and I was the junior professional employed on that day to work on the main scoreboard at The Mote. I got into a terrible muddle trying to keep up with all the wickets that kept falling as Doug shot them out… and I don't think I ever did succeed!

He was also a lovely man. I never saw him cross, and never saw him upset. He was the captain when I first joined Kent in 1954 and he performed heroics for the county in an era when we didn't have the best of sides. When Bryan Valentine and then Les Ames finished, a lot of responsibility rested with Doug, and he never shirked it.

I can also remember seeing Doug, as great a bowler as he was by then, working on his own in the nets. If he was unhappy with the way he was bowling, he used to put a handkerchief down on his ideal length and then spend hours wheeling away in the empty net. That was a valuable lesson to me at my young age.

For Underwood, practice was all about getting himself into the groove, and he would then sit back to concentrate on giving everything on the field of play. On a rain-affected pitch, of course, he was often unplayable - hence his nickname of 'Deadly'. The onset of covered pitches, of course, took those opportunities for complete mayhem away from him - but great bowlers are great bowlers even on the flattest of pitches, and 'Deadly' was no exception.

It pleased me no end, though, late on in his career, when water once seeped under the covers and he got an unexpected chance to bowl again on a rain-affected surface. I was manager of the Kent side by that time, in the early 1980's, and I can still recall the astonishment on the faces of those in our team who were too young to have seen Derek bowl in such conditions before. He completely destroyed the opposition batting line-up, and they were left shell-shocked by Derek's unique combination of pace, turn, lift and - above all - unrelenting accuracy.

In 520 first-class appearances for Kent, Underwood took 1951 wickets at an average of 19.21. Only Tich Freeman and Colin Blythe have taken more wickets for the county, although Underwood can also add a county record 530 one-day wickets to his overall tally. But for his decision to join Kerry Packer's unofficial World Series Cricket, in 1977, Underwood would also have finished with even more than his 297 wickets for England, which came from 86 Tests.

It should not be forgotten, though, that it was that great Kent coach, Colin Page, who persuaded Derek to switch from bowling left-arm seamers to spin. What a piece of advice that turned out to be!

The Fast Bowlers

I have two final places to fill in my select Kent post-War team, and they perhaps present the most difficult of all the selection choices I have needed to make. Kent have possessed a whole host of fine new ball bowlers during the past 50 years or so, and I fear that I am going to have to be quite unkind to some great names!

Nevertheless, my first decision is to ink in John Shepherd at number eight in the order. 'Shep' was a good enough batsman to be classed as an all-rounder, and so his batting ability will further strengthen a formidable line-up and help to protect the tail. But he was also a very fine bowler indeed, with either the new ball or later in the innings, because he had the priceless virtue of being able to swing the ball so naturally away from the right-handers.

'Shep' was also a tremendous competitor, who hated to lose. Although he was Barbados-born, and won five Test caps for the West Indies, he came to Kent as an unknown young player and - like Asif Iqbal - became more than just an overseas player in the hearts and minds of the county's followers. He also truly became 'one of us'.

John represented Kent from 1966 to 1981, and in 303 first-class matches he took 832 wickets at 26 runs apiece and scored 9401 runs - including 1157 in the 1968 season. His all-round value to the team in one-day cricket was also incalculable, and so he really is a 'must' selection for this team!

His selection does mean, though, that I need an out-and-out strike bowler to complete the XI and, for this final place, one fast bowler who is contention is my old friend Norman Graham, who I roomed with on away trips for more than seven years but who only ever went to bed as early as I did on about two occasions! Norman would bowl all day for you, and had great stamina and heart. Who would have thought that this large, very tall man had worn calipers as a child because his legs were not strong enough?

He was, of course, a great socialiser and he claimed to have visited one thousand pubs in Kent during his benefit season! Norman's wonderful benefit result, though, underlined just how highly the Kent public regarded him.

I have also considered the strong claims of the incredibly fast David Sayer, who was up there with Frank Tyson in terms of speed but was such a gentle giant that he used always to pitch the ball up on poor pitches so that he wouldn't hurt anyone, while former England quicks Graham Dilley, Dean Headley, Alan Igglesden and Martin McCague all come into the equation too.

I also must mention Martin Saggers, from the current Kent team, who has performed magnificently in recent seasons and who I hope will continue to take lots of wickets for the county - and get a chance, hopefully, for England.

Then there is Alan Dixon and Alan Brown, who I played with and who were both fine seamers. And what about Richard Ellison, who did so much to help England win the Ashes in 1985 and won 11 Test caps? At his best, indeed, Ellison would be a candidate for my all-rounder's position.

After a good deal of thought, however, I must pick out Fred Ridgway to be this team's spearhead, for the simple reason that his record bears comparison to any of the other leading fast bowlers of his particular generation. Fred only won five Test caps for England, but from 1946 to 1961 his first-class career with Kent saw him claim 955 wickets from 298 matches at an average of 23.81. He was only 5 ft 9 inches tall, but he was genuinely quick and he was still the team's number one bowler when I began my own first-class career in 1958.

A few years earlier than that, when I was just on the staff as a junior, I remember him once refusing to give me my two shillings (the traditional weekly 'tip' for the dressing room attendant, or should I say 'gopher', from each player) because he said I hadn't cleaned his bowling boots properly! But, despite that, I'll still have him in this eleven! He was such a consistently good performer for Kent, and he seldom broke down. That is always a huge asset in any quick bowler.

At this late stage of my selection process, however, I found myself insisting that I should really pick an extra seamer so as to turn my XI into a XII capable of dealing with any pitch or atmospheric conditions that presented themselves on the first morning of a match. To this end, I have somewhat cheekily added Dave Halfyard to the team list. If conditions warranted it, therefore, I could include a third specialist seamer and leave out one of my spinners (difficult though that would be to do!)

Halfyard was in many ways a unique performer - he could hit the seam almost at will, but he also used to slip in a fast off-spinner or a leg-break. For example, I once saw him clean bowl Glamorgan's Gilbert Parkhouse with a googly… which was also just the second ball of the match!

Dave played for Kent from 1956 to 1964, in which time he took 769 first-class wickets at 24 runs apiece. He then suffered broken legs when his three-wheeler vehicle was involved in a crash on the outskirts of Weston-super-Mare, where we were due to play Somerset, and his injuries were so bad that only two men ever thought he would play again.

One was Dave Halfyard himself, and the other was the outstanding physiotherapist Danny O'Donnell, who at that time used to look after both Kent cricketers and Gillingham's footballers. And they were right, as Dave did make it back into the game and played for Nottinghamshire for several seasons.

So, there we are: my best Kent team, from 1945 to the modern day, leaving me with just one more task, which is to appoint the captain. The last task is perhaps the easiest, too, because there will only ever be one Colin Cowdrey… the man I always called 'The Master'.

The 'Lucky' Thirteen

1	Mark Benson	8	John Shepherd
2	Neil Taylor	9	Derek Underwood
3	Chris Tavare	10	Doug Wright
4	Colin Cowdrey (captain)	11	Fred Ridgway
5	Asif Iqbal	12	Dave Halfyard
6	Bob Woolmer		
7	Alan Knott (wicket-keeper)		Manager: Les Ames

Chapter 12
A Word From The President

I had been an employee of the club for almost 20 years before I actually stepped into the Kent committee room at the St Lawrence Ground. This year, as Kent president, I hope to initiate (or, more accurately, in part renew) a tradition where all the playing staff get the opportunity to go into that hallowed area – so as to be able to meet those who run the club on a social and business basis, and to know that they are each a part of the extended family that is Kent cricket.

For most of my own playing days the committee room was, literally, out of bounds to all but the chosen few and their guests. What was accepted was different then, I know, but to us players there was still an unnecessary feeling of 'them and us' that was symbolised by the seeming impenetrability of those four walls.

One of the things I very much want to do in my year as president is to promote even more the 'team' atmosphere in the relationship between the various parts of the club. Committeemen, administrators, marketing staff, players and backroom staff are one big team, and that feeling can strengthen with continued effort to ensure that people get to know and appreciate each other. No only as a former player, but also as someone who has worked in most other areas of the club, I think I am in a good position to take a lead. It is a notable fact, at the moment, that former players like Mike Denness, Chris Tavare, Chris Cowdrey and Graham Johnson are all on the Kent cricket committee. I don't think many other counties can say that about their committees, and it is very noticeable to me, too, that in many cases those former players have returned to the fold despite having left the club under something of a cloud as their playing days came towards an end. That in itself underlines the strength of the Kent cricket family. When I began, there was always a big connection between current and former players, and I'd like that to continue.

In my presidency year, therefore, all the club's players – both first team and youngsters – will at some stage get an invitation to come into the committee room for a drink and a chat at the end of play. It is important for them to meet the committee and officers of the club in an informal way, and it is equally important for committeemen and officials to have the chance to get to know the players better. I particularly want to host such gatherings in the committee room itself, because it is a place where the great history of Kent cricket is so overpowering. How our players perform out there in the middle is vital to everything else that goes on at the club, and it is important to my mind that every player feels the inspiration of that history.

Kent is a very special cricket county, for many reasons. Cricket is perhaps the county's biggest unifying factor, sporting-wise anyway, and people up in Beckenham and Bromley and Bexley are just as passionate about Kent cricket as those down in Canterbury, Dover and Folkestone. That is why the club's recent development of the Worsley Road ground in Beckenham, where a fully-fledged festival week of county cricket and a one-day match against the touring West Indians is scheduled for this coming summer, is so important to the future of Kent CCC. The population numbers in that metropolitan part of Kent make it vital that we have a focal point and a 'shop

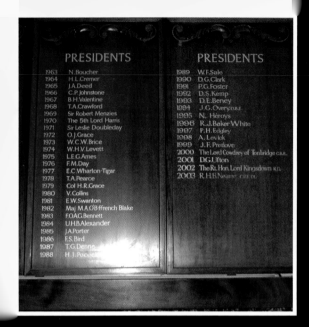

Part of the Presidents' honours board in the pavilion at Canterbury. I have been given the privilege of being next man in

To the victor, the spoils: a selection of the medals awarded to me during my career

I am pictured in the corner of the committee room at Canterbury with some treasured mementos of my career. The caps, from left to right, are Kent second XI, Army, Kent, England and MCC touring cap. Behind are (from left to right) the BBC South East sports award for 2003, the Lifetime Achievement award from Kent for 2003, and a silver salver presented in recognition of my 50 window' in that area. People up there might have a South East London post code, but tens of thousands of them are Kent through and through – and Canterbury is a long way to travel if you want to watch all four days of a championship match.

Over the years, too, a big part of Kent's unique tradition and character has been the policy of the club to take its county cricket to the people, and not just to sit back and expect them to come to it. For most of my career, for instance, we played on nine different grounds and it is a shame that Blackheath, Gravesend, Dartford, Gillingham, Dover and Folkestone have fallen by the wayside. The comparative lack of matches now – there used to be 16 home games in a county championship of 32 three-day matches when I started – is one reason for it, plus of course the increased commercial advantages of playing at Canterbury. The facilities, for public and players alike, are now so much improved at the St Lawrence Ground that it is difficult to take more cricket away from the club's headquarters. And, as I've mentioned at least a couple of times before, what a setting it is! No wonder, during the past two years, it has been voted as English cricket's number one ground in both newspaper and magazine features. At present, too, the Kent club have a vision for the future, in which the redevelopment of the St Lawrence ground will hopefully include, by 2010, a new hotel and conference facility, new hospitality boxes and media centre, new grass practice nets and all-weather floodlit pitches for other sports. More money is needed, of course, for the imminent redevelopment of the Ames-Levett Centre to be followed by this further plan of action. I know what I would spend my first couple of million on, if I won the Lottery!

The surroundings and atmosphere at both the Nevill Ground in Tunbridge Wells and The Mote in Maidstone also contribute much to the overall 'feel' and public face of Kent cricket. Moreover, in addition to our lovely grounds, we have always been a county blessed by excellent crowds, and even in the lean years of the 1950's we never failed to be one of the top three counties in the country in terms of levels of support. The sight of Canterbury, Tunbridge Wells, Maidstone and now Beckenham with hospitality tents up and spectators lining the boundary is very much at the heart of the Kent cricket brand. Indeed, we often get more people turning up to watch second XI cricket at Canterbury than some first-class counties get for their championship fixtures!

They say, too, that there are more than a thousand cricket clubs in Kent, stretching from Blackheath to Tenterden and from Westerham to Margate, and that is another remarkable part of our great cricket heritage. Cricket first flourished in the Weald, of course, but the sport's strong roots in our wonderful part of the world are very visible still. We cannot and must not be complacent, and in Kent I don't believe we are, but I am very hopeful for the future of cricket in this particular corner of England. We have such a tradition, and we must guard it most jealously.

Those who know me are well aware that I am not often lost for words, especially on the subject of Kent and Kent cricket, but I was so overcome with sheer pride on being asked – out of the blue – to be the county club's next president that I did find myself unable to speak for what seemed like quite a while (in truth, it was probably about 30 seconds – but that is a very long time for me!).

Last November my wife Raye and I were invited to go over to the Shepherd Neame brewery in Faversham by Bobby Neame, my predecessor as president, ostensibly to pick up the registration documents for the car which the company had provided for me during the previous four years as part of their sponsorship of Kent CCC. This had been given to me as a wonderful leaving present on my retirement from the club, and I must mention here that Shepherd Neame had also supplied my club car for the last 20 years of my time at Kent.

Anyway, on our arrival at his office, Mr Neame announced that there was also another matter he wanted to discuss with me, and my surprise verged on shock when he then said: "I would like you to follow me as next year's president". My emotions did almost get the better of me, if truth be told, but in the weeks and months that have followed I have become very focussed on what is both a marvellous honour and a tremendous opportunity for me to put back so much into Kent cricket.

Receiving so many letters of congratulation has been lovely for Raye and I, and it has only served to heighten my determination not to let my county down in my presidential year. I am mindful of the fact that despite being the 120th Kent president, in a line stretching back to The 3rd Lord Harris in 1870, I am only the third former professional player to receive this distinction, after Les Ames (1975) and Derek Ufton (2001), but I hope that my status as a former Kent player will prove to be a strength of my term 'of office'. David Fulton, the captain, already knows that I will do all I can to help him and his fellow players feel comfortable and supported as they go on their quest for honours in 2004.

Wouldn't it be nice if the team could bring a trophy or two to Canterbury during this year! That, for me, would be the perfect way for my presidency year to be remembered, because the most important thing of all is the players and the team and what they can achieve out there in the middle. And this current Kent team has some very fine players, led by someone who I feel is in the process of becoming a very fine captain.

David Fulton is extremely dedicated to his job of leading the county, and to my mind has all the attributes he requires to be successful on the field. He is a player good enough to set an example, and he is intelligent and bright. Technically, he is very good and his man-management skills are excellent. He is still growing in terms of his experience in the job, and I believe he has the ability to be one of the best captains Kent have had.

In Robert Key, meanwhile, I see a batsman capable of being one of the very best - if not the best - in this county's history. He has already had a taste of Test cricket, and he is now very much a senior player in the Kent team even though he only turns 25 during the 2004 summer. I hope that he sees himself as such this year, and shows the determination to take the next step up towards achieving real consistency. How good Rob Key becomes is now very much up to him, and I hope he is aiming very high.

Ed Smith proved himself to be a high-class run-scorer at county level last season, and he and James Tredwell went on the National Academy tour of India at the start of 2004. I was interested to see, too, that Tredwell was asked to captain the Academy side, which showed that at the still tender age of 21 he had impressed good judges with his maturity and tactical awareness. As a spinner, too, he has only just begun career-wise, and will certainly get even better with added experience.

In Geraint Jones, Kent have a wicketkeeper-batsman to follow in the incredible Kentish tradition of Les Ames, Godfrey Evans, Alan Knott, Paul Downton and Steve Marsh. There is no doubt in my eyes that Jones is a high-quality performer with both the gloves and with the bat, and hopefully he will be a massive asset to Kent – and perhaps England – for many years to come.

Martin Saggers and Min Patel are both bowlers of proven class, and Martin is a tremendous competitor who always gives of his best. Min has a very important year coming up, after the injury problems which wrecked 2003 for him, and it would be such a fillip for the team if he can make a successful comeback in this his benefit season. With other fine players around like Matthew Walker and Amjad Khan, with several other youngsters of potential, and with two excellent overseas players who have already fitted in very well into the Kent dressing room, I think we have a team that is most capable of challenging for honours.

For the current generation of players it is extremely important, too, that the National League one-day titles of 1995 and 2001 were won. Those trophies in large part exorcised the ghost of the 1970's team, a subject which our successors in the 1980's and early 1990's not unnaturally grew tired of hearing about. But a taste of success, as happened for a number of our current players in 2001, is a vital stepping-stone to greater achievements. As I have said earlier in this book, the great team of the 1970's needed that early 1967 Gillette Cup win, plus the experience of a raft of near-misses, before it truly came of age.

What the present squad can also be proud of, going into the 2004 season, is that Kent are now the only county never to have been outside of the first division of both the championship and the one-day league. That fact underlines the team's status, and consistency of performance, and I was particularly pleased to see the way David Fulton and his players responded to the challenge of hauling themselves back up the table in both those competitions last summer, following a very poor start to the season that was not exactly helped by David's own awful eye injury. In the second half of the summer they played some magnificent cricket, and I hope that the team can start off their 2004 campaign in the same manner.

I have a lot of respect for the way teams of the modern era work so much harder than we did, as teams. There is much more emphasis on the technical side, and of course there are numbers of coaches around now that we just did not have. I am very pleased, too, to see that the main Kent coaching staff for 2004 of Simon Willis, Paul Farbrace and Chris Stone are all very much homegrown and 'Kentish' in their approach and outlook. Going back in time, I was very disappointed – for instance – when Bob Woolmer left us and proceeded to enjoy so much coaching success at Warwickshire and then with South Africa. Producing our own players is very much the Kent way, and long may that continue. Importing is, and can only ever be, short-termism.

With all counties now signed up to the academy system, however, which puts more emphasis on the production of local talent, I remain concerned about increased player movement between counties. The distinction between List One (untouchable) and List Two (approachable) players seems to have grown blurred in recent times. Structure-wise, I applaud the introduction of Twenty20 cricket, which has already created a new enthusiasm for the game at county level, and floodlit matches, but I still doubt the wisdom of dividing the championship into two divisions. With three-up and three-down, especially, it seems to me to be a recipe for negative cricket in the first division and sometimes for too many artificially-created results in the second tier.

There is one aspect of the modern game, though, that I abhor. To my mind, as I have alluded to before in these pages, there is simply no place in the game of cricket for unnecessary sledging or appealing. A truly great fast bowler does not need to swear at or abuse the batsman. He might have an odd word, if it is done in the right way, but all the great cricketers that I played with and against treated their opponents with respect. Sure, they sometimes tried to knock your head off, and they were always ultra-competitive, but why does natural aggression like that have to be accompanied by insults or mockery? Why, too, should we have to put up with mass appealing, which in effect is tantamount to intimidation of umpires and often downright cheating?

These blights on the game were beginning to creep in during my last years as a player, but they have grown far worse over the past couple of decades. In my view, it is the players and especially the captains who should clamp down on it. As I've said before, to be tough and hard is nothing to do with chirping from slip or squaring up to a batsman at the end of your follow-through. Hardness is how you play, hardness is winning the game, and in my experience the toughest of competitors were usually the most generous of opponents in defeat.

I was appalled when, several years ago, Bob Woolmer came up to me at an Old England game being played at Edgbaston and told me about an incident involving one of his young Warwickshire players that had occurred a week or so earlier at Tunbridge Wells. This young lad was making his championship debut against Kent and, on taking guard, he had to put up with a certain Kent player shouting from his position close to the wicket to his fast bowling colleague waiting at the end of his run almost 50 yards away. "Hey, run through your mark and knock his f...........head off". Even more disappointingly, nothing was apparently said to this player either by his captain or by the umpires. I couldn't believe it.

Too much silly chat has filtered its way down to age group cricket. Tom Cartwright, the former Warwickshire, Somerset and England all-rounder, and for many years now one of the best and most respected bowling coaches in the country, tells of a recent under 16 county match involving his own Glamorgan team in which he was asked to stand as umpire because one of the invited officials could not make it at the last minute. After three overs of incessant chatter, especially from the opposition captain, he stopped the bowler in mid run-up and turned to the young lad in charge. "I don't want to hear any more, captain. And if you say another word yourself you will be off the field," said Tom. It all stopped immediately, and everyone simply got on with the game. I wonder why more officials don't do that. Encouragement, and clapping of hands, is fine – but there is no room in cricket for sledging or stupid comments towards the opposition.

One of the fiercest players to face on the field in my early years was Fred Trueman, known universally as Fiery Fred of course. I remember, as a young player, sitting in the Kent dressing room before a match against Yorkshire at Harrogate, and Fred walked in the door as bold as brass and started to point his finger around the room. "One, two, three, four… five. That's five wickets for me today straightaway, then. What about the rest of you!" But it was done in a humorous way, and our senior guys joined in the fun and had a bit of banter with Fred. I just sat there, wondering if I'd been in his original five, or not!

On another occasion, when I was batting against Fred, a Yorkshire fielder at mid-off let a shot go through his legs as he moved across to try to stop the ball. "I'm sorry, Fred, I should have kept my legs together," he cried as he turned to chase it. "Not you, son, your mother!" came Fred's reply, quick as a flash. Everyone within earshot, including us batsmen, laughed out loud. Fred, you see, could always think of something clever or acerbic, and with the ball in his hand he could be downright hostile, but he never indulged in any sledging.

No player I took the field alongside, though, was ever more competitive or motivated than people like Derek Underwood, Alan Knott or Colin Cowdrey. They did it at the highest level for their entire careers, as their combined total of 295 Test caps perfectly illustrates, but they also knew how to behave. Moreover, whenever Derek took a vital wicket or Knotty a vital catch (and there were a fair few of those over 20-odd years!) there was great pleasure shown but no fist-pumping or aggressive poses of triumph. Why do you need that anyway? As a bowler it is your job to take wickets, and as a wicket-keeper it is your job to catch the nicks and stop the rest. Aggression is an attitude of mind, a determination… or at least it should be.

The pressuring of umpires is something the game's authorities really must act upon. About seven years ago I got so incensed with what I was seeing out there on the field that – with Kent's consent – I wrote to John Carr, then the cricket secretary at the Test and County Cricket Board at Lord's. I proposed that, on the condition that in return there would be no dissent from players, the first-class umpires should decree that all batsmen were not to walk. In other words, even the most obvious of nicks or bat-pads should be left to the umpires to rule on. I think all batsmen should walk if they know they're out, but I proposed the opposite because I saw it as the only way the issue could go forward in terms of the umpires' authority being unquestioned again. I had a very nice reply from John, but he feared it could not happen.

I never stood there and disputed the umpires' decision, because there would always be times when you got the benefit of the doubt and it worked in your favour. The only time I stood and looked at the umpire was in a Kent game against Nottinghamshire at Trent Bridge. I attempted a drive but took a big divot out of the pitch with the toe of my bat. There was a tremendous appeal from the keeper and slips, and I was astonished. I could have sworn I had missed the ball by some distance, but Tom Spencer's finger duly went up. My disappointment teetered over into a dissenting look, I'm afraid, before I turned to go, but when I got back into the dressing room I spotted a big red mark right on the bottom corner edge of my bat. That evening, after play, I made a point of going out to meet Tom at the gate, as he came from the field, and said: "Sorry, Tom, my mistake – can I buy you a pint?" Players should concentrate on their job, which is hard enough, and let the umpires get on with theirs. They have very difficult jobs, too, don't forget.

As a postscript to this subject, what about a story which my first coach, Claude Lewis, told me. I think this says all that really needs to be said about all the concerted appealing that goes on, from cover point and square leg as much as from the bowler and the slips. Claude once witnessed a game where the player fielding at mid-off kept appealing for lbw, very loudly. The umpire gave him a few looks, but said nothing. Then, next day, when this player's turn came to bat, he looked down the pitch to the same umpire and asked for a middle-and-leg guard. The umpire merely replied: "Certainly. But would you like me to give you it from here, or from mid-off?"

It is the stories, and the friendships, which mean the most after a long association with cricket, the greatest game. As I said in my introduction, I have been privileged to meet so many wonderful people through the game of cricket. As Kent president, I will relish going around the county on my official duties and I am very much looking forward to travelling further afield as I also have a role to play in supporting the players throughout 2004. I am already determined to visit Worcester, where I made my Kent first-class debut, and to visit Edgbaston, where my friend Dennis Amiss works as chief executive of Warwickshire, and Old Trafford, where Jim Cumbes and Jack Simmons are other long-standing friends of mine.

Tim Tremlett at Hampshire has also sent me an e-mail telling me I must take in the Rose Bowl during my presidential year. Tim will remember a second XI game at Bournemouth where, as a young player, he was captaining Hampshire and I was captaining Kent in my capacity as second team coach. At lunchtime on the final day there was a knock on our dressing room door and Peter Sainsbury, their coach, asked to see me. He said that Tim was thinking about declaring and setting us a very fair target, but that he was worried that I would promote myself up the order from number 10 and lead a run chase! Don't forget, this was in August 1977, and I had been in the England team just two and a half years earlier! I assured Tim that I was only interested in developing my team's young players, and that I would not be moving up from number 10. The result? We collapsed, and I found myself batting for well over an hour as we attempted to stave off defeat! I came in at 154-8 and ended up 73 not out after our number 11 Tony Verrinder, who we called 'Otto Von Verrinder' because he looked just like a German officer with his clipped blond hair, joined me at 214 and we held on to reach 236-9 and the draw.

A very special part of this coming summer will be the Canterbury Festival, which of course is always my favourite time of a Kent cricket season. We are due to be playing Sussex, the reigning county champions, and it promises to be a wonderful match to watch. But, in addition to that, it is my position as president to invite the opposing team's president to the game and entertain him on behalf of the Kent club. It will be a particular pleasure for me, therefore, to be able to welcome my very good friend Jim Parks and his wife Jenny to the Canterbury Festival. I played in Old England matches with Jim for 10 years, which cemented a friendship which had begun during our respective playing days, and Raye and I will be thrilled to have Jim and Jenny to stay with us at home during that period.

I have so many memories from my 50 years in the game that I could easily write another book full of them! No, it's all right… I'll spare you that! But I will begin to wrap things up by telling a few more stories which underline to me the richness of a life in cricket. Like the day my first son, Tim, was born, on July 22 1966.

My first wife Elaine was with me at a Kent match at Maidstone when, on the second evening, July 21, she began to feel that things were happening on the baby front. The nearest maternity hospital was in Minster, Sheppey, so I drove her there and I sat up all night while we waited… and waited. Nothing more was happening, and by coincidence the staff nurse in charge of the unit was a Kent member who recognised me. "Aren't you supposed to be playing in the match at The Mote?" she asked me, in the early hours of the morning. When I said I was, she told me to go back home and try to get a couple of hours sleep, and that she would be on the end of a phone at the hospital if I wanted to ring during the day to check on any progress. So, after a quick nap and a change of clothes, I found myself back at the ground preparing for the final day's play.

It was a game that had been badly affected by the weather, but we had declared and set Worcestershire 192 to win in quite difficult conditions. I rang up just before play began, and then again at lunch, and once more at tea. Soon afterwards, with Worcestershire nine down and on the verge of defeat, I dropped a sitter of a catch at gully off Derek Underwood's bowling. Someone in the team shouted out: "Brian, I bet you your baby has just been born. That's obviously why you have just dropped that catch!" And, five minutes later, after Derek had wrapped up the Worcestershire innings for 159 with his seventh wicket, I was greeted on the boundary edge by the news that there had been a phone call from the hospital – five minutes earlier – to tell me my son had arrived!

As a player, there are always opponents who trouble you more than others and – in my case – it was the great Hampshire and England medium-pacer Derek Shackleton. He used to get me out at least twice every season and, by the end of the 1960's, I was sick of the sight of him. Imagine, then, how my eyes lit up when I read in the newspaper that 'Shack' had announced his retirement! I couldn't wait to face Hampshire the following season, knowing that he would at last not be there to torment me, and as luck would have it the fixture list threw us up against them at Canterbury in the very first championship and Sunday League games of the summer. But what then happened? On the Saturday, which was the opening day of the championship fixture, one of their fast bowlers Butch White broke down and Shackleton was called out of retirement to stand in for him in the Sunday League game the following day! He arrived at Canterbury with time only for a half-hour warm-up before opening the Hampshire bowling. I was facing, and almost immediately I nicked a ball that was going down the legside, trying to glance, and was caught by the keeper. I was out to Shackleton for another duck, just when I thought I'd seen him off!

As you have read, a lot of strange things have happened to me on the cricket field over the years, and experience taught me to expect nothing less. But literally nothing could have prepared me for my final first-class appearance. And no, it wasn't in 1976 when I suffered the broken hand which finished my career. It was in the last week of August, 1985, against the Australians at Canterbury.

I was 46, and coming to the end of my stint as manager of the first team. We had injuries in the squad and most of our young players were in Birmingham preparing for the final of that summer's county Under 25 competition. I arrived at the ground on the morning of the match to discover that three more players were struggling to be fit, and that Graham Johnson – who had recently been informed that he would not be retained by the club – had changed his mind about playing in the match. Graham didn't want to play, and I couldn't even persuade him to change his mind because of the sudden problems of raising a fit XI. In the end, it became apparent that I was the only possible eleventh man, and as I was still registered as a player by the club there was no problem with me slotting in to make up the numbers. Chris Cowdrey, the captain, had no objection but the fun began when the news was announced in the dressing room and that I would be batting at number 10. "Why number 10?" piped up Derek Underwood, with an indignant look on his face but a cheeky grin lurking not far from the surface. "Excuse me, Lucky, but when was the last time you scored a first-class hundred!" Derek, you see, was still fresh from the only first-class century of his career – a triumphant 111 against Sussex at Hastings the summer before – and so he wanted to know why he was still down to bat at number 11!

My last first-class ton had, indeed, come nine years earlier than Deadly's, in 1975, and further evidence that I was now very much a blast from the past came when, early on the second day, I walked out to bat with Kent on 301-8. The crowd gave me a very nice reception, but the Aussies could not believe that here was this old codger striding out to bat without a helmet on. In truth, I wasn't wearing one because I didn't have one, and also because I'd never worn one in my entire career. It would have felt so unnatural. But Craig McDermott, the Australian number one fast bowler, was distinctly unamused and thought I was winding him up! His first ball to me was a bouncer and he followed through up the pitch far enough to give me a stare after I had ducked underneath it. "Good morning!" I said, to which I merely received a grunt in reply. I managed to hang around a little while and made a single in a stand of 25 with Steve Marsh before McDermott had me caught in the slips. Later, there was another amusing moment when McDermott himself came out to bat and suddenly realised that he'd forgotten his box. I walked over from my fielding position to tell him it might be better to forget to wear a batting helmet rather than a box!

Kent lost that game by seven wickets, by the way, after Greg Ritchie and Allan Border made first innings hundreds and we were bowled out for 126 in our second innings, McDermott taking 5-18. But I remained nine not out at the end of it, after battling through 62 minutes at the crease. From a personal point of view it was nice – finally – to take my leave of the first-class cricket stage by testing myself against the Australians one last time… and walking from the field of play unbeaten.

Statistical Record

Brian William Luckhurst

Born: February 5, 1939, in Sittingbourne

Overall first-class career (1958-1985):
389 matches, 22,303 runs, highest score 215, average 38.12, hundreds 48.

Kent first-class career:
336 matches, 19,096 runs, highest score 215, average 37.96, hundreds 39.

Also took 64 first-class wickets at 42.87 and took 391 catches.

Kent one-day career:
149 matches, 5,689 runs, highest score 142, average 43.09, hundreds 9.

Test career:
21 matches, 1,298 runs, highest score 131, average 36.05, hundreds 4.
(plus 1 wicket at 32.00 and 14 catches)

Unofficial Test career (v Rest of the World, 1970):
5 matches, 408 runs, highest score 113 not out, average 45.33, hundreds 1.

One-day international career:
3 matches, 15 runs, average 5.00

And Finally...

I hope that my sons Tim, Simon and Matthew, my wife Raye, who I married in 1985 after my first marriage had sadly ended, and all my other family and friends have enjoyed this account of my 50 years in cricket. I thank them for all their support over the years, and I also thank Kent County Cricket Club for always being there for me since those far-off days of 1954.

I have played my cricket with so many lovely people at Kent, and worked with many more. Besides the players, the backroom staff at the county cricket club – those in the office, groundstaff and maintenance staff – are all key members of the operation. There are and have been many unsung heroes at Kent CCC, and I'm sorry if I've not mentioned you all in these pages.

Thank you, everyone.